The GOSPEL according to ISRAEL

✡ ✡ ✡

A Jewish Presentation of the
Good News of Yeshua the Messiah

KEVIN GEOFFREY

©2025 by Kevin Geoffrey

All rights reserved. Except for brief quotations for the purpose of review or comment, or as quotations in another work when full attribution is given, no part of this book may be reproduced, stored in a retrieval system, or transmitted in any form or by any means—electronic, mechanical, photocopy, recording or otherwise—without the prior permission of the publisher.

P · U · B · L · I · S · H · I · N · G

A ministry of Perfect Word Ministries

www.perfectword.org
1-888-321-PWMI

All Scripture quotations taken from the Messianic Jewish Literal Translation of the New Covenant Scriptures (MJLT NCS), ©2018 by Kevin Geoffrey, and the Sacred Scriptures, Messianic Jewish Literal Translation (MJLT), forthcoming. Some Hebrew names and other words or phrases have been translated into English or simplified for clarity, by permission of Perfect Word Publishing. Verse citations follow Tanakh numbering conventions. Where numberings differ from the Christian Old Testament, the Christian numbers are included in brackets.

ISBN #: 978-0-9837263-7-1

Cover design by Esther Geoffrey
Cover photo by alefbet/123RF, "Gateway to the Ruins of the Fortress of Masada, Israel"

Printed in the United States of America

"But from there you will seek A$_{DONAI}$ your God and will find Him, when you search after Him with all your heart and with all your soul."

D<small>EUTERONOMY</small> 4:29

וּבִקַּשְׁתֶּם מִשָּׁם אֶת־יהוה אֱלֹהֶיךָ וּמָצָאתָ
כִּי תִדְרְשֶׁנּוּ בְּכָל־לְבָבְךָ וּבְכָל־נַפְשֶׁךָ

דברים ד׳:כ״ט

Contents

Preface — vii

CHAPTER 1 **God of Creation** — 1

CHAPTER 2 **God of Judgment** — 5

CHAPTER 3 **God of Salvation** — 11

CHAPTER 4 **God of Promise** — 15

CHAPTER 5 **The God of Israel: God of Deliverance** — 27

CHAPTER 6 **The God of Israel: God of Commandments** — 37

CHAPTER 7 **The God of Israel: God of Atonement** — 49

CHAPTER 8 **God of Faithfulness** — 59

CHAPTER 9 **God of Redemption** — 65

CHAPTER 10 **God of Revelation** — 73

CHAPTER 11 **God of Love** — 81

CHAPTER 12 **God of Reconciliation** — 99

CHAPTER 13 **God of Life** — 113

Epilogue — 127

Appendix: What Is the Good News? — 137

About the Author — 147

Preface

For the last nearly two thousand years, the Good News (the "Gospel") that has been embraced and proclaimed by Christianity has presented an inaccurate and incomplete "Jesus." The message we have heard is that God so loved the world that He gave His only Son to die for our sins—that He rose from the dead, defeating death, so that everyone who believes in Him will have eternal life.

But that doesn't tell the whole story.

Though supreme and sufficient in its *essence*, as a message, it is insufficient in its *context*. It lacks the necessary breadth for conveying the gravity of such a life-transforming proclamation. By its abbreviation—both in its explanation, and in our understanding—we cost it its strength.

In light of how the message of Yeshua (Jesus' actual Hebrew name) has been traditionally misrepresented, then, the Good News may not be entirely what we think. Indeed, it is possibly much different—and, likely, much more—than we have heard. Generally speaking, the Jesus of Christianity arises spontaneously in history, vaguely attached to antiquity, tied to unanchored patterns and prophecies, and incidentally (perhaps even inconveniently) Jewish, with little purpose beyond loving us, saving us, and having a wonderful plan for our life. But such a narrow characterization, cut chiefly from the cloth of the New Testament, grossly ignores the glaring testimony of the first three-quarters of our Bible: the Hebrew Scriptures.

To begin the message of salvation with Yeshua—as consequential and preeminent as He is—is literally to come in near the end. Rather, the message of the Good News of Yeshua is inseparably embedded in the history shared between the God of the universe and His most peculiar people, Israel.

Absent this perspective, the Good News loses both its foundation and its focus. While there can be no doubt that without Yeshua there is no Good News at all—no salvation, no eternal life, and therefore no hope—neither is there any Good News *without the people of Israel… the Jewish people*. Though it may come as a complete shock to most Christians, the Bible—including the New Testament—is not a Christian-centric book, but an Israel-centric one. From Genesis to Revelation—all the way from beginning to end—the Bible does not tell a Gentile story, but a thoroughly Jewish one (one that nevertheless includes and invites Gentiles in). When Yeshua is ripped from this context, there is no longer any tangible basis for someone to trust in the deliverance He promises. Without recognizing the seamless Israeli thread tying the entire tapestry of the Good News together, Jewish people are severely handicapped in locating the means of their salvation, and Christians cannot fathom the dependence of their salvation upon the Jews.

The Gospel According to Israel, then, aims to restore this long-neglected context, and therefore the inherent, inextricable Jewishness of both Yeshua and His very excellent Good News. By returning the Hebrew Scriptures to their proper place in our biblical consciousness, the complete story of Israel receives its due prominence. It causes our view of the so-called Old Testament to go beyond utility for providing background information or prophetic benchmarks, and instead brings Israel into focus as God's seedbed and catalyst for bringing the Good News to the world. Realizing the Jewish people's continuing place in God's salvation plan more fully prepares Jews and Gentiles alike to truly grasp what is entailed in receiving, sharing and following Israel's Messiah.

Whether you are a believer in Yeshua seeking an authentic gospel—for yourself, or to share with Jewish family and friends—or a Jewish person searching for the truth of whether Yeshua is actually Israel's Messiah, I pray that you find within these pages a picture of the Good News that is genuine, biblical, *and Jewish*. May *The Gospel According to Israel* help you reset your perspective, rectify your misperceptions, and lead you into soul-humbling awe of the matchless price our God has forever paid... for you.

Kevin Geoffrey
February 28, 2025

The GOSPEL according to ISRAEL

CHAPTER 1

God of Creation

The Good News starts at the beginning.

> In the beginning, God had created the heavens and the earth: And the earth had been nothingness and emptiness, and darkness... –Genesis 1:1-2a

Before the very spreading out of the heavens and the foundation of everything, there was God, and nothing but God. Without Him there would be no light... no land or seas, no plants or trees. There would be no sun or moon or stars... no day, no night, nor passage of time. There would be no waters teeming with life or creatures filling the sky. There would be no animals of any kind moving and creeping and crawling along the ground. Without God, not a single man, woman or child would have existed, would exist now, or would ever exist—forever. Without God, there would be nothing but "nothingness and emptiness, and darkness."

But "God said, 'Let light be'; and light was" (1:3).

In an instant, all creation began to spring to life. Vegetation and terrains. Planets and luminous bodies. Flying things and swimming things and all manner of things that breathe. The reality of God's eternal power and divine nature at once became the perpetual, unavoidable testimony that *He is*. From out of the void, a limitless and timeless Deity formed a majestic, unending space of boundless wonder. In His magnificent wisdom and ancient understanding, the Creator of the Universe effortlessly "[hung] the earth upon nothing" (Job 26:7); the Maker of everything suspended in the sky the very sun we still see. And in just six days, ADONAI—the God of Israel—made "the heavens and the earth, the sea, and all that *is* in them" (Exodus 20:11). Then on the seventh day, being pleased with all that He had completed, He rested. The God of Creation had commanded everything to be, and the creation heard and obeyed.

> And God saw all that He had done, and look!—Exceedingly Good. –Genesis 1:31

Yet the "Creator of Heaven"—the "Former of *the* Earth"—did "not create it [all] *for* nothingness, *but*... for inhabiting" (Isaiah 45:18). With the foundation laid and the framework established, God painted upon His grand canvas the culmination of His perfect creation:

> And God created the man in His image; in the image of God He had created him... –Genesis 1:27

Out of the lowly "dust from the ground" (2:7), God created man. Through no human effort or will, nor by any random or cosmic accident, the Creator formed the man from a mere, lifeless clump of clay. Set apart and exceptional among all God's creatures, the God-figured man was to be given a unique and solitary spark. And so, having formed the earthen avatar, the Creator then "breathed into [the man's] nostrils *the* breath of life, and the man became a living soul" (2:7).

Then God caused a luscious garden grove to spring forth from the ground, and He set the man there to rest, and to serve and to guard His custom-made creation. Yet when He surveyed all He had made, God saw among them not one creature suitable as the man's companion. So God put the man into a deep sleep, removed one of his ribs, and out of the man's very own body, built for him *a woman* (2:21f). Now a binary humankind—"a male and a female He had created them" (1:27)—it was in this immutable pattern that the man would find a complementary, helpful counterpart. No longer would the man be alone.

For millennia to come, this same God would continue to personally shape and mold the form and innermost parts of everyone. With His own infinite hands, He would weave us together in the protection and warmth of our mothers' wombs (Psalm 139:13). The very One who first animated man would know each of us from before we were ever born (Jeremiah 1:5).

> And God blessed them, and God said to them, "Be fruitful, and multiply, and fill the land..." -Genesis 1:28

"By the spoken word of His power" (Hebrews 1:3), the God of Creation birthed and sustains all that there is. A mere utterance from the whisper of endless eternity had shaken the nothingness and forged it to become everything. And all things could be made this way—"prepared by a saying of God" before the very foundation of the world (Hebrews 11:3, John 17:24)—because also "in the beginning was the Word, and the Word was with God, and the Word was God" (John 1:1). The Voice enunciated in the darkness, His Pronouncement resounded in the void... and as the "first-born of all creation" (Colossians 1:15), He began to speak *life*. Without that prolific Word "not even one thing [would have] happened that has happened" (John 1:3). The Word existed before everything, and then through Him, all things were made. Since before the very beginning of time, He has held the whole universe together (Colossians 1:16-17). For,

> By the word of ADONAI the heavens have been made, and by the breath of His mouth all their host. –Psalm 33:6

The evidence of the unending work of the God of Creation is plain for all to see. And the Life that He gives, He gives abundantly, so that we may live and move and be.

What blessing would humanity then return for such a pure and precious gift? In response to the One who puts breath into the soul of every one of us, how would man then repay the glory due His Maker?

Would the creation honor and love his Creator?

> [T]his people has drawn near *to Me* with their mouth,
> And they have honored Me with their lips,
> But their heart they have put far off from Me...
> –Isaiah 29:13

CHAPTER 2

God of Judgment

The Good News gives us a choice.

The God of Creation had spoken, and through His Word, the heavens and the earth had been made. He filled the world with life that sprawled across the land, sea and air, and—beautiful and pristine—it flourished. As His crowning achievement, God created a caretaker for His creation who would multiply, bless the earth, and be blessed by it in return. God made man in His very own likeness—wholly unique among all His creation—to be the sentient recipient of His abundant goodness. The man was placed into a garden paradise, and for him God created a woman to be his helper. Wholly provided for, the world's first two people were naked and innocent and unashamed (Genesis 2:25). God walked among them in the breeze of the day (3:8), and everything was exceedingly good. For the moment, all things were in total harmony and peace.

But God had also done a most curious thing.

Among the abundant grove of good food-producing trees, in the very middle of the garden, God placed two peculiar species (2:9). One was "the tree of life," the fruit of which would cause the one feasting on it to live forever. The other was "the tree of the knowledge of good and evil"—this one, a banquet of edible death. God specially identified the second tree to the man, and told him, "do not eat of it... [or] you will certainly die" (2:17). And with that, God had issued man his *first command*, with no further explanation provided. The grove—not to mention the tree of life—abounded with choice and desirable fruit, so there was no good reason to even approach that other, illegal growth. All the man had to do in order to obey his Creator was to freely partake of the abundance of the garden—and to leave the one, forbidden tree alone.

Yet the allure of the prohibited proved to be wily competition, and the *first temptation* would soon find its prey. The forbidden tree was deemed "good for food" and "a pleasure to the eyes"; the knowledge of good and evil, it seemed, was "desirable to make ONE wise" (3:6). Casting doubt on the Creator's credibility, the woman — at the leading of a certain serpent — began to question if what God had said was true (3:1). So the wife and her husband took of the forbidden fruit. The *first sin* was born from an appetite for the taboo.

God had given the man a command, and He gave it in the context of a kind of *covenant*. God's implied promise to provide the man with "every tree of the garden" was offset only by His requirement that he refrain from just one of them (2:16). As part of this covenant, God also laid out the consequences the man would face should he choose not to comply—suggesting only blessings for as long as he obeyed. So while the man had God's word and all the benefits of His creation, in return, God only wanted the man to keep His command.

"But the sin, having received an opportunity through the command, brought about all covetousness" (Romans 7:8) within the newly formed souls. Had there been no command to defy, the tree might have gone largely unnoticed, lost in a lush forest of nourishment and delight. But the lure of the forbidden—urged on by a crafty Adversary and Accuser—led them to distrust their Creator, take the word of a snake, transgress the covenant God made with them (Hosea 6:7), and enact its fatal provision. It is a progression that has since been repeated by all people for all time:

> Afterward, the desire (having conceived) gives birth to sin, and the sin (having become fully-grown) brings forth death. –James 1:15

Though not immediate, the promised death was now imminent (Genesis 5:5). But first came the flood of sweet, succulent knowledge.

Instantly, "the eyes of them both were opened, and they knew that they were naked" (3:7). Now robbed of their innocence, their ill-gotten awareness did not yield the wisdom they had coveted. Instead, they gained the knowledge of the *first fear and shame*. Recognizing the sound of their Creator in the garden, the man and his wife tried in vain to hide from the One who made them.

In a matter of moments, man's close-knit relationship with God was unraveled. What had been a peaceful harmony—God and His creation both inhabiting the same space and time—was now broken and dissonant, enduringly scarred by sin. Immediately, man sought *separation from God* as a remedy for his fear—estrangement as a solution for his shame. God had given the command and forged His covenant, and He now had no choice but to keep His word.

In a last, desperate attempt to avert disaster, the woman turned on the serpent, the man turned on the woman, and the flesh of humankind proved its corrupted state. The first fear and shame gave way to *the first excuse and blame*, as they were unwilling (or unable) to take responsibility for their wrongdoing.

With special affliction assigned to that instigating serpent,[1] God then proceeded to curse the whole creation He had entrusted to the man. As for the misleading woman (1 Timothy 2:14), she would now be pained in childbirth and subject to the authority of her husband; while the man, for listening to another's voice over God's, would now eat by the sweat of his own brow and be sustained by the work of his own hands. Marked by *the first shedding of innocent blood*, God properly covered and clothed His children with animal skins (Genesis 3:21), and then drove them out of the garden. That perfect place, created to be enjoyed and protected by the man, would now be guarded from him forever. With the covenant broken and the man's separation from God complete, the garden's tree of life was no longer within reach. The man would indeed one day return to dust. The God of Judgment had passed His sentence.

In the beginning, God's world was perfect and pristine. The man, Adam, had only to trust in what his Maker said and remain unseparated from Him in order to live and be cared for forever. But when God gave the *first command*—embedded in the *first covenant*—and Adam gave in to the *first temptation*, then "through [the] one man the sin entered into the world, and through the sin, the death" (Romans 5:12). All creation had come under the curse of God's covenantal judgment. God had given Adam his life, but also His word that if he should

---

[1] Genesis 3:15 is considered by many to be the first Messianic prophecy, though it lacks specificity and corroboration in the New Testament.

choose not to listen to and trust His voice, then there would be dire, irreversible consequences. That *first sin* led to the entire creation's disconnection from its Creator. "The judgment indeed *is* of one *man's misstep leading* to condemnation" (5:16). Adam—from whom we have all descended—caused his own separation from God; God merely enforced it.

> But your *causes of* guilt have made a separation
> Between you and your God;
> And your sins have hidden
> *His* face from you—from hearing *you*.
> –Isaiah 59:2

We share Adam's fate, then, because we share his same weaknesses—his same susceptibility to temptation and propensity for sin. We fear and hide and separate ourselves from God, violating the covenant with our Creator and bringing judgment upon ourselves.

The God of Judgment has barred everyone access to the tree of life by the garden gate forever. If only He had made another way...

> For even as in Adam all die, so also in the Messiah all will be made alive... –1 Corinthians 15:22

CHAPTER 3

God of Salvation

The Good News rides on a perfect rescue vessel.

Adam had brought sin into the world, soiling God's pristine creation. The misstep of the one man caused death to reign for all—the result of disobedience and self-separation from the Creator. Forced to follow through on His covenantal obligation, God enacted His judgment and barred mankind from everlasting life by way of the garden tree. Through his own disobedience, the man was cast away from the presence and provision of God.

As time went on, the descendants of Adam—in their long-separated state—floundered and grew increasingly distant from their Maker. Realizing the full potential of their depravity, they became violent and corrupt, imagining and thinking nothing but evil in their hearts. God saw the abundant wickedness of man—that His most glorious creation had grown into His greatest source of grief. With His heart broken at the degeneracy of His masterpiece, ADONAI became "sorry that He had made man" (Genesis 6:5-6).

Anguished that the flesh of man had corrupted the earth, God resolved to do the unimaginable... and start over. He determined that He must wipe out all life from the face of the earth—not just the life of men, but of every living thing upon the ground. Though such punishment seems incomprehensible, the reality is that mankind was already hopelessly lost. Without the swift and severe intervention of the Creator, all men for all time would be doomed to death forever. So with a mixture of staunch judgment and intense regret, ADONAI set out to deprive man of his continued existence and "destroy[] them with the earth" (6:13). The wickedness of man had run its course; all creation stood condemned...

...and yet, the God of Salvation did not leave humanity stranded.

While all of mankind stood apart from God, one man—Noah—"found *unmerited* favor in the eyes of ADONAI" (6:8). This "righteous man" had somehow escaped the evil of the world and was "perfect" among his generation (6:9), being "seen *as* righteous" before the face of God (7:1). Though in his flesh Noah was an inheritor of Adam's curse, his character caught God's attention—and He was pleased. For as it was with man at the beginning in the garden, Noah "had walked habitually with God" (6:9), and had fellowship with Him. God knew from His walks with Noah that this was a man who would obey Him and do "all that [He] commanded" (7:5). Through Noah, ADONAI could redeem His creation; in His grace, God would establish His covenant (6:18).

So God declared to righteous Noah that "an end of all flesh [would be] coming" (6:13)—that He would soon bring a cataclysmic Flood to destroy the earth and everything that moved and breathed upon it (6:17). Then God instructed Noah to build for himself a great vessel in which to harbor and ride out the approaching storm. By an enormous ark, Noah would escape the coming judgment and administer the rescue of earth's creaturely remnant.

Sprawled out over the equivalent of one and a half football fields, encasing two million cubic feet with wood and pitch, the ark carried specimens from every kind of animal of the air and on the ground of the earth, all gathered by Noah. By twos and sevens he brought them in, filling to the brim his soon-to-be-floating refuge. At God's behest, and with both faith and fear (Hebrews 11:7), Noah brought also his household—his wife, and his sons, and their wives. "Eight souls" (1 Peter 3:20) to keep humanity alive; one divine lifeboat to save the world.

Through the opening on the side of the ark, Noah and his brood entered the narrow doorway to salvation, and when they had fully come in, Adonai closed it behind them (Genesis 7:16). Then "all *the* fountains of the great deep" broke open, and the deluge of the heavens burst forth (7:11). From all directions—from above and beneath—the waters spilled out, seizing and raising up the ark to safety. But as the violent waters covered the mountains, all that drew breath in the grave of the earth died and were wiped away.

> Only Noah was left, and those who were with him in the ark. –Genesis 7:23

For the next twelve months, Noah remained shut up in the ark as the waters receded and the ground became dry in the newly remodeled world. When he finally emerged, "every living thing, every moving thing, and every flying creature" on earth came out with him (8:19). Noah immediately built an altar and made sacrifices to God, who received to Himself the aroma as a sweet fragrance. And God declared in His heart that though "the heart of man *is* evil from his youth," never again would He cause such destruction on their account (8:21).

God blessed Noah and his sons and told them to "be fruitful and multiply and fill the earth" (9:1), and He established His covenant with them, promising He would not again send a flood to destroy His creation (9:9ff). And with His everlasting covenant, God gave the magnificent sign of the rainbow—that whenever He places that perfect prism in the mist of the sky, He will be reminded of His promise, and we of His awesome judgment and abundant deliverance.

Though the imaginations of man's heart are only evil (6:5), the Good News is that the God of Salvation is still willing to save. Knowing that the flames of violence and sin would keep burning in the flesh of His creation, God still chose to initiate His redemption plan, so that man's hope for life would not be extinguished forever. By rescuing Noah and establishing His covenant with him, God set a precedent for the way He would now deal with man's condition. No longer would all mankind be left to its depravity and sin; God would make a Vessel to serve Him and carry forth His salvation.

The God of Judgment judges harshly, but the God of Salvation saves by making a way out. Though He knows how evil we are in our hearts, He is still willing to preserve us and redeem us from eternal destruction. The covenant with Noah closed the door on global watery destruction, yet it did not guarantee man's eternal safety. Through Noah, mankind received salvation, but how would humanity handle its second chance?

God used a "perfect" and "righteous" child of Adam to begin reconciling His relationship with man. Yet by what righteous One—through what narrow door, and upon what perfect rescue vessel—may Noah's descendants be raised up to the unending salvation they do not deserve?

> By faith, Noah… prepared an ark to the salvation of his house… and became heir of the righteousness according to faith. –Hebrews 11:7

CHAPTER 4

God of Promise

The Good News keeps its commitments.

Because the descendants of Adam had become earth's sinful citizens, God destroyed the world. Oath-bound and grief-stricken, the Creator washed away His creation, cleansing it in the waters of a purifying, violent Flood. Yet above that deluge, God lifted up Noah to save a remnant of life from the face of the earth. Through the narrow doorway to a lifeboat of grace, God had preserved humanity in one righteous soul. ADONAI was initiating His long-suffering redemption plan for the heart of sinful man, and with a covenant, He began to prepare the way by which anyone could be saved.

According to God's blessing, the sons of Noah were fruitful and multiplied. Yet the generations of Noah's descendants were disobedient, rebuffing God's word to spread out and "teem in the earth" (Genesis 9:7). As they remained together, migrating as a group and increasing in number, Noah's nomadic kin eventually came to settle on a plain where they built dwellings of brick and mortar. Enamored by their technology and abilities, they had in mind to construct an enormous city, and within it, a tower that reached to the heavens. They sought to satisfy their pride by making a name for themselves, firmly entrenched in their refusal to disband. But God saw the city and the tower, and that the people were united in their efforts to glorify and fortify themselves. So Adonai confused their language such that they could no longer understand one another, and—in fulfillment of His intended design—He scattered them all across the earth (11:9).

The dispersed people of the earth continued to multiply. Ever increasing in the diversity of their ancestral lines, the prideful progeny of Adam and Noah divided into numerous nations. For ten generations after Noah, God bided His time... until the day when He would pluck one ordinary, flawed human being from obscurity, selected seemingly for no special reason at all. Out of a world of nations separated from God and one another, the Creator would continue His reconciling work by setting apart one unremarkable man—one peculiar people—for Himself.

God of Abraham

Abraham[2] was hardly a peasant, yet he lived in his father's household, on his father's land, for the first seventy-five years of his life. Surrounded by a large extended family, Abraham was married, though his beautiful wife Sarah was barren and unable to have children. One day, with no advance notice or preface of any kind, Adonai came to Abraham, telling him to leave his father's house for another land which He would show him. And, unquestioningly, Abraham did as he was told, having received God's amazing promise:

> "And I will make you become a great nation, and I will bless you and make your name great; and you will be a blessing. And I will bless those blessing you, and him

---

[2] Abraham and Sarah were born Abram and Sarai, but God later changed their names (see Genesis 17:5 and 17:15).

who is despising you I will curse, and blessed in you will be all the families of the earth." –Genesis 12:2-3

The man with no children would "become a great nation." The descendant of those who had desired a name for themselves would himself have his name made great. And the blessing or cursing of all the families of the earth would rise or fall on the treatment of him and his seed. In return for these promises, God required of Abraham precisely... nothing. God's covenant with Abraham (Acts 3:25) had commenced. All Abraham had to do was go.

So Abraham took Sarah, along with everything he owned and the people who served in his own house, and they left the land of his father. Having brought him to the promised land, God covenanted with Abraham (Genesis 15:18) that it would one day belong to his descendants—that his seed would be more numerous than the dust of the earth and the stars in the sky (Genesis 12:7, 13:14-15, 15:5, Acts 7:5). Though they found the land already inhabited, and old-aged Abraham yet had no heir, he believed in ADONAI—the God of Promise—and ADONAI considered his faith as righteousness (Genesis 15:6).

After living for more than two decades as immigrants in that promised land—with, apparently, no word from God—ADONAI appeared and broke His quarter-century silence over the matter of the unfulfilled covenant. Abraham, now nearly a hundred years old, fell on his face as ADONAI reiterated His promise of land and innumerable, uncountable descendants (17:1ff). And "at the promise of God, [Abraham] did not stagger in unbelief, but was strengthened in faith... having been fully persuaded that what He has promised He is also able to do" (Romans 4:20).

By an inconceivable conception—through the laughable and the ludicrous—God then chose to open ninety-year-old Sarah's empty, ancient womb. The seemingly absent God of Promise would surely live up to His word, for, even in the deadness of the womb, "is anything too wonderful for ADONAI?" (Genesis 18:14).

> And ADONAI did to Sarah as He had spoken. And Sarah conceived and bore a son to Abraham in his old age, at the appointed time.... And Abraham circumcised Isaac his son—BEING a son of eight days—as God had commanded him. –Genesis 21:1-4

God of Isaac

Isaac, sealed by the covenantal sign of circumcision, marked the beginning of Abraham's promised line and the distinction of a set-apart people. Until this time, Abraham had proved himself most malleable. But now, with the coming of his son Isaac—the promised progenitor of Abraham's name—would the father of many nations continue to obey, even in the face of great personal loss?

When Isaac, much-loved by his father, had grown into a young man, God spoke to Abraham with what anyone would perceive as an appalling request. As a test, God instructed him to take Isaac and sacrifice him as a burnt-offering (Genesis 22:2); He commanded Abraham to kill his own son. For what felt like forever, Abraham and Sarah had waited for their promised heir. Would God now break His word and take away that which He had sworn to give? Was He testing Abraham to see if he believed that God would raise his son from the dead? Yet without a word of objection—with no resistance whatsoever—the very next morning, Abraham set out in obedience to his God.

Abraham and Isaac traveled for three days to the mountain where God was waiting. Placing the wood for the sacrifice on Isaac's back, Abraham took the fire and the knife, and they started up the mountain. Unable to foresee his apparent peril, Isaac nevertheless recognized the elements for a sacrifice, and noticed the conspicuous lack of a lamb. Upon inquiring of his father concerning the absent animal, Abraham cryptically—if not faithfully—replied, "God will see *to* a lamb for Himself for a burnt-offering, my son" (22:8).

But despite Abraham's assurances—to himself and to his son—what followed next would surely cut to the heart of any father... and that of his trusting child. Having arrived at the place which God had told him, Abraham proceeded to build an altar, place the wood upon it, and lay his son Isaac—bound—on top of the wood (22:9). Foreshadowing the willingness of another Father to give up His one and only Son, righteous Abraham—without hesitation, without a sound... indeed, without a doubt—took the knife in his hand, and readied himself to run through his beloved, faithful Isaac.

Suddenly, a voice from the heavens rang out, stilling the hand of collected and compliant Abraham. "Do not send your hand into the boy, nor do anything to him, for now I have known that you are fearing God and have not withheld your son—your only one—from Me" (22:12). And when Abraham lifted up his eyes, he saw a ram with its horns stuck in a thicket. In place of his son Isaac, the God of Promise had indeed provided a Lamb—and Abraham saw Him, and rejoiced (John 8:56-58).

The test for Abraham was not simply to see whether or not he would obey the most painful—the most horrific—command imaginable. Rather, God tested Abraham to see if he would continue to believe in and stand by the promise, even if God's word were called into question—even if the promise appeared unquestionably broken. The righteous man would not doubt God's word despite God Himself seeming to give him reason to doubt it. Abraham's pliability and composure were not detriments of his character, but attributes of a faithful man to whom a faithful God could commend His promises.

Because Abraham proved his faithful obedience—confirming his selfless willingness to hold back nothing from God—God swore, and He blessed, and He recertified His promise that by Abraham's incalculable descendants, a chosen nation would rise and be a blessing to all the peoples of the earth (Genesis 22:16-18). God would keep His word to Abraham, repeat His blessings to Isaac, and renew His covenant with that model of a sacrificial son. Soon the heir of Abraham would have a covenantal son of his own, and, like his father, be responsible to maintain that separate and unique ancestry. The nation of Abraham would continue to be blessed by the God of Isaac... all because a father listened to—and obeyed—the voice of the God of Promise.

> And ADONAI appeared to [Isaac] during that night, and He said, "I AM the God of Abraham your father. Do not be afraid, for I AM with you, and I have blessed you and will multiply your seed because of Abraham My servant."
> –Genesis 26:24

God of Jacob

Before he died, Abraham found a wife for Isaac from among the people of his father. He was determined to maintain his line's distinction while still sojourning in that promised, yet foreign, land. Isaac loved his wife Rebekah, who, like Sarah, had also been barren. But Isaac prayed to God, and his prayers were abundantly answered: Rebekah conceived and had not one child, but twins (25:21-22). From the womb, the two boys contended with one another, for God, indeed, had already made His plans (Malachi 1:2-3). Esau, ruddy and hairy, came out first; and clutching his heel was relentless Jacob, the supplanter.

Isaac was partial to Esau, the hunter and man of the field, and —as the firstborn son—heir apparent to the promise. Yet Esau could not see past the needs of his present circumstances. Despising his birthright, he sold it to his younger brother for a mere saucer of stew (Genesis 25:34). Then, when Esau was ready for marriage, he took foreign wives who brought a bitter spirit to Isaac and Rebekah (26:35). But despite the misery this created in Isaac's house, Isaac loved Esau and intended to pass on his blessing to him.

So when Isaac grew old and had become blind—knowing that death drew ever nearer—he asked his beloved son Esau to hunt some fresh game, prepare and cook it for him, and then receive his blessing. Rebekah, however, being partial to Jacob, devised a plan to undermine her husband and take matters into her own hands. Perhaps seeing that the covenant was in jeopardy, or perhaps just being distressed by Esau's choice of wives (27:46), Rebekah surreptitiously approached Jacob with the details of her underhanded scheme. Having already usurped his brother's birthright, Jacob willingly heeded his mother's bidding. And after deceiving Isaac with a hot meal and an Esau-like disguise, he took the blessing reserved for his elder, unwitting brother (27:35).

When the truth came to light, Isaac and Esau were severely distraught—with Isaac being visibly and violently shaken. Branding Jacob a cheater and hating him in his heart, Esau was overt in his intentions to kill his deceptive brother. Rebekah and Isaac, seeing that Jacob was in imminent danger, urged him to run away to the house of his maternal grandfather. And with an apparent realization that God's will was for his second-born, Isaac blessed Jacob with a covenantal blessing: that God would bless him, make him fruitful, give him the blessing of his father Abraham, and cause Jacob—the son of the birthright—to carry on the covenant, and possess the promised land (28:3-4).

Jacob ran. That night as he slept, he saw in a dream a stairway[3] reaching up to the sky, with angels of God ascending and descending upon it (28:12). When he looked, he saw ADONAI standing at the top of the stairs, calling out to him and declaring,

> "I AM ADONAI, God of Abraham your father, and God of Isaac. The land on which you are lying, I give it to you and to your seed. And your seed will be as *numerous as the dust of the earth*.... And all *the* families of the earth will be blessed in you and in your seed. And look! I will BE with you, and will guard you wherever you go, and will cause you to return to this land. For I will not leave you, even to *such time* that I will have done that which I have spoken to you." (Genesis 28:13-15)

Though Jacob had bargained for the birthright of his brother and deceitfully taken the blessing of the firstborn, God made no mention of it, nor spoke any chastisement against it, but readily joined Jacob to the covenant of his fathers. Undoubtedly, Esau had rejected his legacy, caring only for the blessing of prosperity and power—which he ultimately lost. God, it seems, prefers a faithful supplanter to a self-centered, wayward son.

---

[3] Or ladder

When Jacob awoke, he was in awe of all he had witnessed in the dream. So he set up a stone as a standing pillar, poured oil upon it, and made a vow before the God of his fathers Abraham and Isaac: since God promised to be with him, to guard him on his way, and to one day return him home, then ADONAI—the God of Promise—would be his God too.

> And Jacob lifted up his feet, and he went toward the land of the sons of the east... –Genesis 29:1

A changed man, Jacob the deceiver became Jacob the shrewd, and he found a wife he loved from among his father's kin. Having lived in that land a long time, Jacob's family life was not without its share of drama—and his added wives and children were multiplied with it. Finally, after twenty years and eleven sons, God told Jacob it was time to return to his father's land (31:3). He set out, full of fear about his return (32:10-12[9-11]), but God would soon prove to him the man he had become.

One night on the journey home, having prayed and sent his flocks and family on ahead, Jacob remained alone. Suddenly, Jacob found himself intensely wrestling with a mysterious man for the remainder of the night. As dawn was breaking, so was Jacob, for the man—seeing he could not prevail against Jacob—touched Jacob and injured him. But stubborn Jacob would not let go, holding out—once again—to be given a blessing. In reply to Jacob's fears and lack of confidence, the struggle revealed to Jacob the truth and tenacity of his character. That morning, the man not only blessed Jacob as he had demanded, but gave to him a new name. And Jacob the Supplanter was reborn Israel the Relentless, for he had "persevered with God and with men, and prevailed" (32:29[28]). When questioned by Jacob, the man refused to reveal his name, yet Jacob knew he had been face to face with God, and his life had been delivered.

The God of Salvation had given the world a second chance through Noah; now the God of Promise began to repave the way to life as the covenant-God of Abraham, Isaac and Jacob. In hope against hope—through endless waiting, old age and barrenness—Abraham believed the promise that he would become the father of many nations. So in his being tested, Abraham offered up Isaac—"the one and only son, who received the promises"—believing by faith that God was able to give back life "even out of the dead" (Hebrews 11:17-19). Isaac, too, by faith, blessed Jacob "regarding coming things" (11:20), realizing that God's promises can be as hard as they are true. And in Jacob, God bore abundant fruit—choosing not just a man, but, one day, a nation to change the world—so that all the families of the earth could find faith, *and find Him*, through the peculiar people of the promise.

Great struggles yet awaited the fledgling people of Abraham's line; nevertheless, his faith would leave an inheritance far beyond the offspring of Jacob. Though Abraham, Isaac and Jacob all "died not having received the promises" in full, in faith, they had "seen... from afar" (11:13) the countless souls of other ancestries—"those of faith—[who would also be considered as] sons of Abraham" (Galatians 3:7-8). Because of Abraham's trust, and the promises that God made with His covenant people, the promise of life is "*made* sure to all the seed" (Romans 4:16). The God of Abraham, Isaac and Jacob opened the door to life through inconceivable, unbelievable faith. The legacy of salvation is passed on by the God of Promise—He who is "bringing the dead to life, and is calling the things not being as being" (4:17).

By faith, Abraham, being called, obeyed to go out to a place that he was about to receive for an inheritance, and he went out, not knowing where he was going. By faith, he sojourned in the Land of the promise as a strange country, having lived in tents with Isaac and Jacob, fellow-heirs of the same promise. –Hebrews 11:8-9

CHAPTER 5

The God of Israel: God of Deliverance

The Good News finishes what it begins.

Having dispersed Noah's descendants to form a world of nations, God continued His reconciling work through obscure, unremarkable Abraham. God covenanted with Abraham that He would make him into a great nation, give him a great name, and make him a blessing to all the families of the earth. God also promised Abraham a land as a possession for the generations that would miraculously be born through him. And even though he had no children and was personally given no inheritance in the land—"not even a footstep" (Acts 7:5)—Abraham believed God. The covenant made by the God of Promise was renewed with Abraham's son Isaac, and again with Isaac's son Jacob...

...the promise, however, would not come without pain.

Even before Abraham first became a father, God gave him the bad news.

"Know certainly that your seed will be a sojourner in a land not theirs... [and that nation] will have afflicted them *for* four hundred years. But the nation whom they serve I also will be judging, and after this [your seed] will go out with much property..." –Genesis 15:13-14

Abraham's promised progeny would take a necessary detour from the blessings of the promised land to be afflicted in a foreign one—and this for almost half a millennium. Yet it would not be Abraham, nor Isaac, who would see God's word come to pass. Rather it would start with Jacob—whom God named Israel—and his twelve sons.[4] The people of Israel would go into bondage, but the God of Israel—the God of Deliverance—would bring them out.

Jacob returned to the land of his father Isaac, where his sons would work the pastures as shepherds. But of all his children, he most loved his eleventh son, Joseph (37:3)—a fact not hidden from Joseph's many older brothers. They were therefore jealous of Joseph (37:11) and hated him (37:4), so they betrayed him and sold him into the land of Egypt. "But God was with [Joseph], and delivered him out of all his oppressions, and gave him favor and wisdom," such that Pharaoh, the king of Egypt, made him governor over all the land (Acts 7:9f). When a great famine came, reaching even the land of Israel, Jacob and his family grew desperate. And so the sons of Israel went down to Egypt for food, finding Joseph in charge—not just of the storehouse, but of their fate. Yet what the brothers of Joseph had long before devised for evil, "God devised it for good" (Genesis 50:20). For it was not his brothers' betrayal that had sent him into Egypt, but the God of Deliverance, "to preserve life [and] to place a remnant of [Israel] in the land... to give life to [the house of Israel] by a great escape" (45:5,7,8a). Welcomed by Pharaoh and invited to Egypt, Jacob joined his

---

[4] Jacob had a twelfth son after he set out to return home.

son and deliverer Joseph in a *land of deliverance*—though not the one promised to his fathers. So on the way, God reassured covenant-carrying Jacob, echoing His promise to Abraham,

> "I AM God, the God of your father. Be not afraid of going down to Egypt, for I place you there to *make you into* a great nation. I Myself will go down with you to Egypt, and I Myself also will certainly bring you *back* up." −Genesis 46:3-4a

And so the seventy souls[5] of the house of Jacob went down to Egypt, fulfilling the word of God to Abraham and trusting the covenantal faithfulness of the God of Israel.

Moses, Servant of God

Israel settled in Egypt in the land of Goshen, and they were fruitful and increased greatly in number there—just as God had said they would do. Jacob, Joseph, and all his brothers eventually died (Exodus 1:6), and soon another king arose over Egypt. This new king, however, had not known Joseph (Acts 7:18), and was therefore uneasy about the rapid expansion of this strange people on his sovereign soil (Exodus 1:9). So this Pharaoh enslaved the people of Israel, working them severely with bitter, hard labor (1:11ff). And for more than three centuries, the people of Israel endured their cruel and harsh enslavement...

...until the time had finally arrived for God to raise up another deliverer.

The king at the time continued to be gravely dissatisfied with the Hebrews' multiplication—despite their imposed, oppressive conditions—and in a genocidal act of heartless popula-

---

[5] LXX and Acts 7:14 say seventy-five

tion control, he ordered his Egyptian subjects to drown all of Israel's newborn sons in the Nile (1:22). But one defiant Hebrew family was unwilling to allow the slaughter of their beautiful infant son. When his mother could hide him no longer, she set him in a basket on the river, that it might sail him to a better destiny (2:3). As his older sister followed along the shore, the basket landed in the reeds near the daughter of Pharaoh. Recognizing the child as one belonging to the Hebrews, she sent him back—unknowingly—to his own mother for nursing (2:6ff). After the child was weaned, he was returned to the daughter of Pharaoh, who took him as her own, named him Moses (2:10), and raised him in the wisdom and power of Egypt.

For forty years (Acts 7:23), Moses lived as an Egyptian in the palace of the king, yet he was not unaware of his camouflaged Hebrew origins.[6] And upon encountering an Egyptian beating one of his own Hebrew brothers, Moses finally snapped (Exodus 2:11f). Perhaps agitated and torn from decades of seeing his people's cruel treatment, it was only a matter of time before he could bear it no longer. Moses killed that Egyptian, and then—though he was not afraid (Hebrews 11:27)—he fled under the death-threat of Pharaoh (Exodus 2:15). Soon finding himself in the land east of Egypt, there Moses would marry, have children, and live quietly for a lifetime (2:21ff)...

...but the God of Deliverance was hardly done with Moses. God had heard the cries of Israel, and had not forgotten His covenant people (2:23-24).

After forty more years, when Moses was eighty (Acts 7:30), one day he was out, as usual, shepherding his father-in-law's flock

---

[6] Implied in Exodus 2:11. Also, he knew of his brother Aaron (Exodus 4:14).

on what turned out to be the mountain of God (Exodus 3:1). All at once, ADONAI suddenly appeared to Moses in a burning fire, engulfing a nearby bramble in flames—though the bush was not consumed. And there for the first time, ADONAI spoke to His servant Moses from out of the blazing bush, declaring,

> "I AM the God of your father, God of Abraham, God of Isaac, and God of Jacob.... I have certainly seen the affliction of My people... and I have heard their cry... for I have known their pains. And I come down to deliver them out of the hand of the Egyptians and to cause them to go up out of the land... to a land flowing with milk and honey.... [S]ay to the sons of Israel: 'I am' has sent me to you." –Exodus 3:6-8,14

To assimilated Moses—his whole life spent at a distance from who he truly was—God immediately identified Himself as the covenant-making God of Moses' Hebrew people Israel. With Moses, and with those who were yet enslaved in Egypt, ADONAI would rekindle His promise to Abraham, Isaac and Jacob, and make this now innumerable people into a great nation. In pledging to bring them out from under the burdens of the Egyptians and to deliver them from the service of slavery, ADONAI had but one, sole intention: to fulfill His covenant and preserve His chosen people—through whom the world would one day be restored to Him.

God then told Moses to go down to Egypt to demand the release of His people. But He also said that the king would not comply until he was supernaturally compelled. And so Moses the chosen one (Psalm 106:23)—doubtful and resistant (Exodus 4:1,10)—took up his shepherd's staff and his family, and set out to deliver a message... and a people.

Remembering the Promise

Moses obeyed God, and when he arrived in Goshen, he declared the word of "I am" to the elders of Israel, doing wondrous signs for them so that they would believe (4:30-31). With his people primed to receive their deliverance, Moses went in to Pharaoh—to the den of his former life—and announced boldly to the king,

> "This *is* what ADONAI, God of Israel, has said: 'Let My people go... that they may serve Me in the desert.'"
> –Exodus 5:1, 7:16

But just as Moses had been warned by God, Pharaoh did not let the people go. And so the king hardened his heart and, in the face of Moses' impudence, caused the already abused people of Israel to suffer even further (5:7). The hardship of their labor was increased, and they were beaten by their brutal taskmasters (5:14). As their misery and affliction escalated, the people turned and blamed their deliverer (5:21), leaving Moses disillusioned and not a little testy toward God (5:22ff). Yet to Moses' complaints, ADONAI responded not with conciliation, but with an ancient account of a long-forgotten promise.

> "I *AM* ADONAI, and I appeared to Abraham, to Isaac, and to Jacob.... And I also had established My covenant with them, to give to them... the land of their sojournings.... I have also heard the groaning of the sons of Israel... and I remember My covenant." –Exodus 6:2-5

God attached His covenant with the patriarchs Abraham, Isaac and Jacob to His attention toward the people of Israel. In so doing, ADONAI was indicating the kind of deliverance He was about to bring. God then made an audacious claim, incorporating the people into that ancient obligation. He told Moses to say to Israel that,

> "I will deliver you [and] redeem you by an out-stretched arm, and by great judgments, and will take you to Myself for *My* people, and I will be to you for *your* God... And I will bring you in to the land which I had [sworn] to give [to] Abraham, to Isaac, and to Jacob, and *I* will give it to you *for* a possession. I AM ADONAI." –Exodus 6:6-8

Though the grip of hardship and slavery had been tightened for a time, the God of Israel—the God of Deliverance—would come and collect His people, and finally fulfill His covenant.

So ADONAI shielded His covenantal people as He sent Moses to do great signs and wonders in the Land of Egypt. He turned the Nile to blood, which the magicians of Egypt mimicked... but Pharaoh would not let the people go (7:15ff). He caused the land of Egypt to be overrun by frogs, prompting Pharaoh to ask Moses for prayer... but he would not let the people go (7:26[8:1]ff]). He turned every speck of Egyptian dust into gnats, agitating and besieging the people, but Pharaoh's heart was exceedingly hard... and he would not let the people go (8:12-15 [16-19]). He sent swarms of insects to invade every home and room in the kingdom, and Pharaoh ever-so-slightly began to budge... though he would not let the people go (8:16-25[20-29]). He wiped out all of Egypt's livestock with a deadly disease, but Pharaoh's heart remained hard... and he would not let the people go (9:1-7). He caused the Egyptians' skin to break out in excruciating boils, but Pharaoh exalted himself against the children of Israel... and he would not let the people go (9:8-12,17). He sent fiery hail to rain down on Egypt, destroying their fields and breaking every tree, such that Pharaoh confessed his sin and pleaded for mercy... yet even then, he would not let the people go (9:25-28,33). He blanketed the land in ravenous locusts that they might devour whatever the hail had not destroyed, but Pharaoh refused to humble himself... and he would not let the people go (10:3-6). He covered the whole land for three days in a thick, tangible darkness, provoking Pharaoh to threaten Moses with death should he ever come before him again... and he still would not let the people go (10:21-28).

> And Moses said, "You have spoken rightly—I will not see your face again." –Exodus 10:29

Deliverance from Slavery

That night, God again revealed a Door of salvation — one through which the world could someday be reconciled to Him. As Moses had instructed, Israel's young and perfect lambs were slaughtered. The people painted the entryways of their homes with that innocent blood, which would serve as a sign for ADONAI to *pass over* their dwelling places and spare them from Egypt's final plague (12:13,21ff). All night long, a great cry rang throughout the land. The subjects of Egypt wailed in anguish as ADONAI carried out His terrible judgment, slaughtering all the firstborn of that national, oppressive power (12:29ff). And at the coming of the dawn, Egypt's broken king relented to the God of Deliverance... and he finally let the people of Israel go (12:31).

Released by shattered Pharaoh, the twelve tribes of Israel emerged from the darkness of generational captivity and stepped into the light of their newfound freedom and peoplehood. Six hundred thousand men on foot — along with their innumerable wives and children (and not a few stray Egyptians)—hurriedly left the only homes and land they ever knew. With them were all their livestock, their uncooked bread, and the abundant plunder of Egypt (12:36)—just as God had said—and before them went Moses, the man of God, following none other than God Himself, who led them in a pillar of cloud by day, and a pillar of fire by night (13:21). Never once leaving them along the way, God took the people into the desert, guiding them to the edge of an impassable and fateful Sea...

...but it did not take long before Pharaoh had a change of heart.

The king resolved to bring back his wandering slaves and, in pursuit of his possession, emptied Egypt of its chariots, horses and army. With the forces of Egypt on one side and the pathless sea on the other, Moses turned toward the waters and stretched out his hands. The people stood speechless as they watched their amazing God split the sea in two, causing the waters to wall up on the left and right, making a way straight through (14:21-22). Walking on dry ground, the people of Israel safely traversed that watery passageway, as Egypt's armies—heading into the sea—continued their pursuit. But on the other side, Moses again stretched forth his hands, and God released the waters. The sea came crashing down upon the full strength of Egypt, and Israel was delivered from Pharaoh's hand forever (14:26-28).

As foreseen in their forefather Jacob, Israel had endured their first struggle with man, yet prevailed—for the God of Israel had seen their suffering and had not forgotten His covenant. God's plan to reconcile the world to Himself and reestablish the pathway to life was now marked by acts of awesome power, and coated with the sign of innocent blood. The people of Israel—now the countless, covenantal children of Abraham, Isaac and Jacob—had become the bearers of God's reputation and the example of perseverance in pursuit of God's promise.

By the hand of a deliverer, Israel had been brought down into Egypt for her salvation; and by another deliverer's hand, she was brought back out. Soon, in the fullness of time, the God of Deliverance would once again send a Deliverer to save Israel...

...indeed, to save the whole entire world.

> My strength and song is Yah, And He became my salvation. This *is* my God, and I glorify Him—God of my father, and I exalt Him. –Exodus 15:2

CHAPTER 6

The God of Israel: God of Commandments

The Good News comes with instructions.

The Creator of the Universe had long been at work to restore mankind from their self-induced separation from Him. Having chosen a people through whom He would make that Way, God set the sons of Abraham, Isaac and Jacob on their promised path. The following four-century journey of salvation and pain would lead them down to foreign Egypt in favor. And though it would also permit their oppressive enslavement there, God would still remember and fulfill His unbreakable covenant to Israel's fathers, and multiply His people ten-thousand-fold. Out of their misery and suffering, God raised up reluctant but faithful Moses to confront Pharaoh and deliver Israel from bondage through powerful, supernatural acts and wonders. And by the shedding of the innocent blood of the lamb, the God of Deliverance saved Israel from Egypt's national, deathly judgment and mightily set His people free.

With Pharaoh's armies behind them at the bottom of the sea, the people of Israel stood on the shores of liberty, about to face the most painful part of their true journey. Finally free from the old, outward enemy, they would nevertheless find they had failed to leave their inner slaves behind. Just three days into their desert pilgrimage, their deliverance had already become a distant memory.

After walking for days and finding only unpotable water, the people complained to Moses, "What will we drink?" (Exodus 15:24)—as if the cloud of God was not standing right there. But God made the bitter water sweet, so that thirsty Israel might drink. Traveling on from there, the people grew hungry and grumbled again at their deliverer. "Oh, that we had died by the hand of ADONAI in the land of Egypt... in our eating bread to the full—for you have brought us out to this desert to put [us] to death with hunger" (16:3). But God made it rain bread from heaven, so that hungry Israel might eat. And again, when they were thirsty and had nothing to drink, the people quarreled with Moses and grumbled more intensely against him. But God told Moses to strike the rock so that, from it, the thirsting flock might again be refreshed, and cease their whining and challenging and testing of their Shepherd (17:7). But though that spiritual Rock would follow and supply them wherever they would roam (1 Corinthians 10:4), the people would not be dissuaded from their lingering doubts about this God.

Six weeks after the last Hebrew foot had tread on Egyptian soil, the community of Israel finally arrived at the base of the mountain of God. Weary from their exploits, the people made camp, while Moses went up to learn the message that God would have him deliver. To self-willed, chosen Israel, God was about to define their purpose in the world, and give them exactly what they needed to fulfill it. Framing their national definition in the context of their recent deliverance, God told Moses to say to Israel,

> "You have seen that which I have done to the Egyptians, and that I carried you on eagles' wings, and I brought you in to Myself. And now, if you will truly listen to My voice and will guard My covenant, then you will be to Me a distinctive treasure more than all the peoples—for all the earth *is* Mine. And you yourselves are to Me a kingdom of priests and a holy nation." –Exodus 19:4-6

God had delivered the people of Israel so that He could bring them to Himself and make them a "distinctive treasure" among all the nations.[7] Keeping His long-standing promise to Abraham, God had grown, rescued, and set apart Israel—but not for some baseless elevation of one people-group over the others. On the contrary, God chose Israel as a *servant* and *mediator* to facilitate humanity's restoration back to Him. The reconciliation of God's ancient relationship with man was now finally taking shape. As planet Earth's "holy nation" and "kingdom of priests," God had chosen and ordained the nation of Israel to help save the entire world.

All they had to do was obey.

The Words of the Covenant

To her newly stated national definition, thirsty and hungry and temperamental Israel was instantly resolute in her response: "All that ADONAI has spoken we will do" (19:8). And with that resounding, unalterable voice of conviction and commitment, the people consecrated and washed themselves, complied with the instructions not to touch or approach the mountain, and quietly awaited further instructions from their God.

---

[7] Also in Deuteronomy 7:6-8

Suddenly, on the third day after they had come to the mountain, the sky cracked open, streaming forth bolts of blinding lightning and bowling downward the deafening roars of thunder. The people trembled uncontrollably throughout the camp as they watched the dark, thick cloud settle upon the mountain, and heard the alarming, unsettling sound of the ram's horn (19:16). Engulfed in smoke, the mountain shook violently (19:18). The shout of the horn kept growing louder and stronger. And as ADONAI descended upon the mountain in a blaze of fire, Moses spoke to the God of Israel—the God of Commandments—who answered in the people's ears with thunderous, bellowing blasts (19:19).

The Voice identified Himself as Israel's powerful deliverer (20:2), commanding that they must never force Him to compete with another object of worship—that His love for Israel was a jealous one, so He must not be replaced by "images" of their own making (20:3-6). He commanded them to do nothing that would ever make His reputation empty and void (20:7), and He told them to remember and rest in Him as the world's Creator through their special setting apart of every seventh day (20:8-11). He required them to honor their parents (20:12), and never to murder (20:13); He prohibited them from ever committing adultery (20:14), or stealing (20:15), or answering deceptively against another person (20:16). And He forbade them from desiring things for themselves that already belonged to someone else (20:17). With these ten glorious "words," God established His instructions for Israel—a covenant of "Torah"[8]—concerning how they must behave toward and regarding their God, and how they must act toward and regarding one another. To be

---

[8] Deuteronomy 5:2, "ADONAI our God has made a covenant with us at Horeb"; that is, at Sinai.

that holy, priestly mediator that would help restore the nations to their Creator, Israel needed to love the one true God—with all their heart, all their soul, all their might, and all their understanding—and to love one another as themselves (Deuteronomy 6:5, Leviticus 19:18, Matthew 22:37-40). Love like this would be the fullness of God's instructions (Romans 13:10), bringing eternal life to those who would do it (Luke 10:25-28).

But could they?

When the people saw and heard all this, they moved and stood far off from the base of the mountain, crying out to Moses, "Do not let God speak with us, so that we will not die" (Exodus 20:19). But Moses, turning toward the people to reassure them, explained that God was not so concerned about their bodily demise as something else even more deadly: "Fear not, for God has come in order to test you, and so that the fear of Him may be before your faces, so that you will not sin" (20:20). Then Moses drew near to the thick darkness where God was, in order to receive more instructions for His chosen people. From commands concerning sexual immorality to social responsibility to the institution of a God-celebrating, agriculture-governing calendar, ADONAI laid out to Moses His statutes and guidance for making a sin-resistant, global mediator out of Israel. As for His part, God promised to be Israel's champion—to guard them mightily and defeat all the adversaries ahead of them in order to bring them victoriously into the promised Land. When Moses returned and relayed God's commands to the people, twice more, with unwavering certitude, "all the people answered *with* one voice and said, 'All the words which ADONAI has spoken we will do... and will obey'" (24:3,7). Then Moses wrote everything down in the Book of the Covenant (24:4-7), built an altar, offered sacrifices to God, and enacted with blood the covenant between the people and their God.

> "Look! the blood of the covenant which ADONAI has made with you, concerning all these things." –Exodus 24:8

God then called Moses back up to the mountain, where he waited for six days. All the while, the glory of God dwelled there, appearing to the people as a consuming fire (24:17). On the seventh day, God summoned Moses into the middle of the cloud (24:16), and he remained on the mountain for forty days more (24:18). There, God would give Moses the two stone tablets of the testimony—written by the finger of God Himself (31:18)—and the elaborate instructions and patterns for what was to be the magnificent and glorious earthly representation of His heavenly Tent of Meeting. From among His holy nation of mediators, God then selected a single, chosen tribe to internally mediate between Himself and Israel—a reflection and pattern of Israel's national purpose to the world. And from that tribe, God established the line of Moses' brother as Israel's set-apart, priestly intercessors. In this way—by the creation of the Tent, the setting apart of Moses' kin, and the establishment of the priesthood—the God of Commandments would have a holy, worthy, sacred place to "dwell among the sons of Israel, and... be their God" (29:45).

Before Moses departed from the mountain, God also included details concerning the daily sacrifices, the atonement for sin, and the seventh day as a sign of God's holiness. Finally, God presented Israel's law-giver with the testimony's tablets of stone. He was all but ready to head down the mountain to deliver God's instructions to His faithful and obedient people...

...but Moses had been gone just a little too long.

Disobedience, Wrath and Mercy

What the man of God heard next must have been at least momentarily incomprehensible to him. God would now give Moses the worst news he could possibly receive. During his forty-seven-day absence from base camp, the people had "sinned a great sin" (32:30) and "done corruptly" (32:7), having "turned aside quickly from the way that [God] had commanded them" (32:8). With the willful and ignorant assistance of Israel's soon-to-be high priest, the people threw off their oath, cast their gold earrings into the idolatrous shape of a calf, bowed down to it, and made sacrifices before it. Then unfaithful, unloving, disobedient Israel triumphantly announced, "These *are* your gods, O Israel, who brought you up out of the land of Egypt" (32:4). Then they laughed and sang and danced.

Somehow keeping his composure, Moses then witnessed the promised wrath of his jealous God. In a fiery zeal, God declared disloyal, ungrateful Israel "a stiff-necked people" (32:9), and revealed His intention to consume and destroy the entire nation He had so recently saved. Remaining in check—at least, for the time being—Moses made a moving appeal for God to turn back from the heat of His rage (32:12). Though Moses himself had reason to be furious—having been the target of his own selfish, stubborn people's antagonism—he nevertheless managed to quench the fire of the covenant-keeping God of Commandments:

> "Why, O Adonai, must Your anger burn against Your people, whom You have brought forth out of the land of Egypt with great power and with a strong hand?... Be mindful to Abraham, to Isaac, and to Israel, Your slaves, to whom You had sworn by Yourself, and to whom You spoke, 'I will multiply your seed as the stars of the heav-

ens, and all this land, as I have said, I will give to your seed, and they will inherit *it* forever.'" -Exodus 32:11,13

God's wrath was appeased by the remembrance of His eternal covenant with the patriarchs of His people: God would not fail or forget His promise. So upon assuaging the burning anger of Israel's Deliverer-God, Moses took up the stone tablets in his hands and the word of God in his heart, and he warily descended the mountain.

As Moses neared the camp and began to see and hear the sights and sounds of sin rising from the people, his own rage finally kindled within him, and he threw the tablets out of his hands, shattering them to pieces at the foot of the mountain (32:19). The events that followed are as perplexing as they are unsettling, for when Moses arrived in the camp, he immediately burned up the golden calf, ground it into powder, scattered it upon the people's water, and forced them to drink. Moses then stood at the gate of the camp and called out to the people, "Who *is* for ADONAI?" (32:26), and all the sons of Moses' own tribe flew to his side. Then Moses, according to the word of the God of Commandments, sent the men into the camp to purge and purify Israel—to slaughter their very own brothers, friends and relations. And that day 3,000 men—instead of the whole community of Israel—died (32:28).

Though the embers of God's anger toward Israel would continue to smolder, He nevertheless remained close with Moses, speaking to him "face to face, as a man speaks to his friend" (33:11). He instructed Moses to chisel out two new stone tablets, and at His command, Moses ascended the mountain. God, too, once again descended in the cloud and stood there with him (34:5). Then the covenant-keeping God of Israel passed before Moses, and made His unambiguous and astonishing proclamation: toward His own stiff-necked people, He would forever be

> "ADONAI—compassionate and merciful God, slow to anger, and abundant in *loving*-kindness and truth [to those loving Him and to those keeping His commands],[9] keeping *loving*-kindness for thousands, taking away guilt and violation and sin (but *who* will certainly not acquit, charging the guilt of fathers on *their* children, and on their children's children, on a third GENERATION, and on a fourth)." –Exodus 34:6-7

The God of Commandments would be as merciful as He would be severe. He would be as forgiving as unforgetful. Not powerless, but almighty; not mute, but explicit. This God would not tolerate the violation of His commands—the committing of sins. He would communicate His instructions to His people clearly, and then hold them accountable. His love would extend as far and deep as His wrath would burn hot and high. Israel's love of God, expressed through obedience to His commands, would be all that would determine which extreme His people would receive.

Was this merely a power-hungry God, commanding obedience and love through the threat of punishment and death? How could anyone ever gain full assurance of hope with such a consuming and volatile love? Would a people who had already proven themselves incapable of keeping commands ever cause their sins to be forgotten forever? Was holiness and death and sacrifice really the only way to save the world?

Moses would spend the next forty days with God on the mountain recreating the tablets, writing "the words of the covenant

---

[9] Deuteronomy 7:9

—the Ten Words" (34:28). When he reentered the camp with the two new tablets, he gathered the people and at last gave them all the instructions that the God of Commandments had given him.

As they remained at the mountain's foot for the next seven months, the people would devote themselves continually to the construction of the Tent of Meeting, the forging of its implements, and the fashioning of the holy garments for the priests of Israel. Finally, on the first day of the first month in the second year (40:17)—just shy of one year since their momentous Exodus from Egypt—Israel set up the Tent, along with everything in its courtyard, and consecrated her mediators just as God had said. And the cloud of the God of Commandments "covered the Tent of Meeting, and the glory of ADONAI had filled" it (40:34)—Israel's God was pleased with Israel's lawgiver, His dwelling place, and His people.

After four hundred and thirty years, God had finally established His multiplied, covenantal people, and had given them their singular covenantal commands—something far different and significantly more exacting than anything He had ever done before. He did this not to set aside the promises he had made to Abraham, Isaac and Jacob, but rather to guarantee their fulfillment. Like their set-apart ancestors before them, Israel needed to become righteous. In His infinite wisdom in dealing with an infinitely stubborn people, God gave Israel these instructions—this Torah—"on account of the sidestepping" of His will they had quickly shown they were inclined to do. These special directions were given so that Israel would find its identity and fulfill its purpose of being a national mediator for the world. They were given to ensure that "the Seed to which the promise had been made would come" (Galatians 3:17-19).

In giving Israel such extensive, specific instructions, the God of Commandments knew that they—like us all—would inevitably disobey. But "where the sin abounded, the *unmerited* favor overabounded" (Romans 5:20), giving God the opportunity to accomplish something truly life-saving—something the sinful people of planet Earth would never deserve and could never do for themselves. These commands for Israel, though unyielding, intricate, all-encompassing and required, are nevertheless holy, righteous and good (7:12,14). And yet, they would not be the ultimate means of making Israel righteous (3:20-22). In being zealous for this Torah (Acts 21:20), Israel would be aiming at its climactic, perfect Goal (Romans 10:4)... one they would not see for more than a thousand years.

Israel's long and trying journey into the desert was about to recommence. But the God of Commandments would first preview for His people the atoning sacrifice for the world.

> My tongue sings of Your spoken word,
> For all Your commands ARE righteous.
> Your hand is for a help to me,
> For I have chosen your precepts.
> I have longed for Your salvation, O ADONAI,
> And Your Torah IS my delight.
> May my soul live, and may it praise You,
> And may Your judgments help me.
> –Psalm 119:172-175

CHAPTER 7

The God of Israel: God of Atonement

The Good News requires endless sacrifice.

The Maker of everything had made His choice: humanity's national facilitator of restoration would be the groaning, ungrateful, stiff-necked people of Israel. In fulfillment of His covenant with the patriarchs, the God of Abraham, Isaac and Jacob had delivered His holy people through astonishing feats of power, and given them His commands of love with the sobering assurance of either abundant mercy or glorious wrath. In terrifying displays of authority, the God of Commandments—through His faithful law-giver Moses—made clear Israel's objective and definition as a distinctive treasure among all the nations. As God's priestly servant and mediator, Israel was required to live in faithful submission and obedience to His word. But for the people of Israel to fulfill their uniquely ordained mission of helping to save the world, they first needed to be shown the method and the means of dealing with their own sin, and to find the way of righteousness that would accomplish their own reconciliation.

With their literal and figurative journey still before them, the fledgling nation's principal activity for more than half a year centered on the holy construction of the Tent of Meeting and the subsequent establishment of Israel's picture of purpose: *the priesthood*. What God had designed—and the people implemented—would not merely be a sanctified space served by a specialized society within Israel, but the physical representation of Israel's collective, heavenly vocation on behalf of the entire world. The gloriousness of the Tent and eminence of the priesthood would reflect the weight and substance of Israel's whole reason for being.

Despite the plethora of rigid commands to which God demanded Israel's absolute adherence, for the construction of the Tent of Meeting, He would instead rely on the community's freewill involvement to fill in the framework of His design. Made with the voluntary contributions "from every man whose heart impel[led] him" (Exodus 25:2), this sacred housing was to be built for God by only the most skilled craftsmen. They would fashion and furnish the Tent using the choicest of precious metals, fabrics, skins, woods, spices and stones—illustrious and worthy elements of "an example and shadow of the heavenly..., greater and more perfect tent" (Hebrews 8:5, 9:11). Within the most holy place—set apart by a colorful veil of fine linen (Exodus 26:31ff)—would be a gold-overlaid chest to hold the tablets of the testimony, complete with its angelic cover. From above it, God would then speak with Moses and give him the commands to announce to His set-apart people (25:10ff). Beyond the veil, where the priests would continually serve before God, would be the holy place with its spectacular furnishings—a gold-coated table, along with plates, dishes, bowls, and a lampstand, all of pure gold (25:23ff). In the large courtyard outside this holy tent would be the sacrificial altar and the bronze basin for washing, with a vast length of beautiful embroidered curtains surrounding the entire area (27:9ff). And mirroring the grandeur of the tent itself, the priests would also be arrayed with precious stones and specially spun fine-linen garments for wearing in God's presence—a custom set of clothing all the way down to the sacred, linen undergarments (28:3ff). This intersection between the temporal and eternal—depicting Israel's national, salvific purpose—would become the extravagant setting of God's magnificent, unspoiled space both for meeting with humanity, and for His chosen priesthood to perform their conciliatory, covenant-sustaining work.

It was within this sublime atmosphere that the priestly line, descended from Moses' brother, would assume their anointed office and receive their appointed place within the community. Performing a myriad of functions, such as adjudicating legal matters and overseeing ritual purification, their primary purpose as intermediaries between Israel and her God would be fulfilled through the administration of *the sacrificial system*. Since Israel had now received the righteous regulations of the Torah, any violation of God's distinctions between right and wrong would be afforded "an opportunity through the command" to cause even greater transgression (Romans 7:8). The commands codified not only God's particular instructions for His set-apart people, but an unambiguous knowledge — both generally and specifically — of what God considers *sin*. The sacrificial system was included within these commands in order to deal with the inevitable and habitual problem of Israel's missteps...

...because sin—that ancient separator between God and man—still required a remedy.

In order to satisfy the covenantal requirements under which God could legally forgive the violation of His word, the God of Commandments provided the long-awaited mechanism for making peace and bringing reconciliation with the sons of

Adam. For Israel, that mechanism would be realized through the people's sacrificial offerings—personal possessions paid as compensation for their individual acts of sin and overall sinful condition. By bringing their offerings to the unapproachable God by way of His approachable priests, God, in turn, would forgive the people, make them clean, and cover over the stain of their sin—He would grant them *atonement*.

The Blood Which Makes Atonement

As the first anniversary of the Exodus drew near, while Israel remained at the mountain, God proceeded to detail through Moses the patterns and particulars of the priestly, propitiatory order (Leviticus 1:1ff). The edible offerings brought by the people — serving also as food for the priests — often included various combinations of grain, flour, bread, oil, spice, salt and wine. Yet most of the different types of offering-payments were those of *animal sacrifice*, ranging from the less expensive turtledoves or pigeons to the larger and increasingly more costly sheep, goats and bulls. The people were invited to make voluntary offerings as acts of devotion to express thankfulness (7:12) or to make a vow (7:16). But when God's commands were broken—resulting in sin—only a sin offering would suffice.

The requirements for the sin offering would vary in detail and intensity, depending upon the type and severity of the sin. To begin with, God made provision for *unintentional sins*—for when someone would do "SOMETHING AGAINST one of all the commands of ADONAI his God... through inadvertence" (4:22). Distraction, forgetfulness, or carelessness, then, would be no excuse, for guilt would still be accrued. And yet, in the event a person sinned but "had not known *it*" was sin (5:17), God's mercy would lessen the penalty—though a penalty would be exacted nonetheless.

The sin offering was also prescribed as a remedy for *specific sins*, such as the failure to come forward with eyewitness testimony (5:1), or for uttering a rash or thoughtless oath—either for good or evil (5:4). God singled out specific acts that violated His commands as warranting special attention and treatment at the altar. He also allowed for more lenient penalties—a bird for a lamb, a sack of flour for a bird—for those who could not afford to pay full price.

But perhaps the most punitive of the sin offerings was demanded in cases of deceit, pilferage and oppression of a fellow member of the community. God considered these sins and others like them to be *unfaithful acts against Him* (5:21-22[6:2-3]). Such sacrifices would require not only the highest-priced, lenience-free sin offering itself, but complete restitution to the victim *plus some*. While all sin would be considered to have netted some degree of guilt, not all sin, it seems, was created equal.

And still, regardless of the motivation or offense behind bringing the animal sacrifices, even the least of them was, in many ways, a gory—albeit humane—butchery. Brought before the priests, each fowl would have its head wrung off without separating it completely from the neck, its feathers removed, and its carcass torn open by the wings. For each mammal, they would slit its throat, strip off its skin, flay open its body, cut it into pieces, and wash its entrails. Eventually, the animal's fat, kidneys and liver would be placed upon the fiery altar in order to thoroughly burn them up, while its remaining parts would be set aside for the tired and hungry mediator's meal.

But the grandest mayhem—and greatest gift—was wrought not by the copious slaying and dismemberment of guiltless animals, but by the shedding and emptying of those volumes of innocent blood: sprinkled in front of the holy place's veil; placed on the altar's horns; drained and poured out at the base of the pedestal; thrown and splashed against its sides. And although each individual's offerings never failed to yield the necessary, crimson fluid, the sacrifices hardly stopped there.

In accordance with their divinely commanded duties, the priests would also offer two lambs every single day—twice as many on every seventh. More than twenty times a year, they would add to the slaughter seven lambs, two bulls, a ram, and often a goat. And during the great, annual fall Feast—in a descending mass of flesh and blood—they celebrated the life sustained by their covenantal God through the sacrifice of seven goats, fourteen rams, seventy bulls, and ninety-eight lambs (Numbers 29:12ff). Each year, hundreds if not thousands of blameless beasts—incapable of understanding, much less of misdeeds—were offered up to God to pay a price they never owed: the cost and consequences of human frailty and sin.

The sacrificial climax of Israel's year, however, would be absent the activity and presence of the people (Leviticus 16:17). On that holiest of days, the high priest—by himself, on his own—would enter silently into the sacred enclosure and, through the death of just three innocent animals, perform his most solemn and essential duties. Having splattered the blood everywhere and on everything in that set-apart place, the high priest would then lay his hands on one of the animals' heads, and "confess over it all the guilt of the sons of Israel and all their violations in all their sins" (16:21). Despite every voluntary and sin offering of the people—after a year's worth of extensive bloodletting and dissections—there still remained souls that needed cleansing and sins that needed covering. For the time being, this ceremony's uncommon, priestly work would be the best all-encompassing remedy for sin—yet merely "a shadow of the coming good things" (Hebrews 10:1). The lone high priest had made "atonement for himself, and for his house, and for all the gathered of Israel" (Leviticus 16:17)—one mediator, one payment, one cleansing, one reconciliation.

The God of Israel requires blood for sin because "the life of the flesh is in the blood" (17:11) and "the wages of the sin is death" (Romans 6:23). Inasmuch as sin, disobedience, and violation of God's commands incur a deathly deficit—just as it did in the beginning—the God of Atonement has assessed that that debt can only be paid with blood; that is, *with life*. This is why "with blood, almost all things are purified... and apart from blood-shedding, forgiveness does not come" (Hebrews 9:22): because "it *is* the blood which makes atonement for the soul" (Leviticus 17:11). Yet in order for sinners to be saved from paying with their *own blood*—with their *own lives*—the merciful, covenantal Creator provided a remedy whereby the blood from a sinless life could be accepted as payment for another's sins. And since, among mere men, "there is none righteous, not even one" (Romans 3:10)[10]—such that no one is without sin—God allowed for the substitution of blameless, spiritless animals to be that surrogate life. Yet because of the nature of those "same sacrifices that they continually offer" (Hebrews 10:1)—be it a voluntary offering, a sin offering, or that of the annual day of atonement—such work could only ever serve as a reminder (Hebrews 10:3) that the problem of sin cannot be solved...

...not as long as the mediator—who has sin of his own—must use "*the* blood of others" to make atonement (9:25).

---

[10] Also, "there is no *one* doing good, not even one" (Psalm 14:3, 53:2[1])

No matter how many innocent animals are slaughtered, and oblations are made, and vats of blood are shed, "it is impossible for *the* blood of bulls and goats to take away sins" forever (10:4). And still, this is not even the biggest problem where it comes to sin...

...because there are *some* sins for which the God of Atonement did *not* deem fit to supply a substitutionary animal sacrifice.

For the murderer, the adulterer, the sexually deviant—even the despiser of parents[11]—that one's "blood *IS* on him" (Leviticus 20:9). For these sins *and many other kinds of arrogant acts of defiance against God's word* (Numbers 15:30f), the God of Israel offers no counteragent—no antidote—but instead demands... *death*. Such offenses have exceeded God's mercy and incurred His promised wrath, leaving the violator with no recourse or appeals. In these cases, which Moses enumerates in explicit detail, only the life and blood of the offender is sufficient payment for his violation. For this one, the sacrificial system has no cure; in God's evaluation, no offering-payment will suffice. There is, therefore, *no* forgiveness, *no* cleansing, *no* covering of sin, and *no* atonement. Such a soul has *no* hope — he is permanently cut off from the salvation that comes from reconciliation.

What, then, can be done? Can we ever truly be saved from sin and death? How can we find a lasting appeasement from God's wrath—especially when we have crossed that uncrossable line?

---

[11] murder (Exodus 21:12, 21:15; Leviticus 24:17; Numbers 35:16ff), adultery (Leviticus 20:10ff, Deuteronomy 22:24), sexual deviance (bestiality, Exodus 22:19; homosexual acts, Leviticus 20:13), despiser of parents (Exodus 21:17, Leviticus 20:9)

The Blood Which Conquers Death

The God of Israel gave His people a set of instructions to teach and prepare them to fulfill their unique purpose as His one-and-only, priestly, mediating nation. That Torah made Israel subject to a penal code, as well as a sacrificial system, through which the God of Atonement could legally provide His people a pathway to peace whenever they transgressed His established boundaries between right and wrong. It also called for the creation of a holy, undefiled, extravagant depiction of heavenly mercy—a space where God could meet with His anointed intermediaries and transmit forgiveness and atonement through them to His people. And though it called for the bloody, repeated and extensive taking of innocent life, and furnished no positive outcome for perpetrators of capital crimes, it was nevertheless essential to the covenant with Israel—another door through which God's people would enter, in furtherance of His plan for the reconciliation of the world. This method and model of requiring blood for life would serve as a divine template for something even greater and more perfect, so that people's sins—all sins—could finally be taken away.

The deficiency of the sacrificial system is not in its divine design, but in the unlimited depravity of man, the limited absolution of its priests, and the naturally restricted effectiveness of their offerings. Because while those mediators would have been able "to sympathize with our weaknesses," they were nevertheless "tempted in all things likewise *as we are*," so that none of them could remain "apart from sin" (Hebrews 4:15). God's holy priesthood—those responsible for the work of making atonement—were subject not only to the defilement from their own sins, but to the eventual deathly end that sin's high price demands (Romans 6:23).

But what if the loving, gracious and merciful God of Israel—the God of Atonement—decided to send Someone *better*?

Such a priest would not simply need to be good, but *perfect*—one who could promise life, and not be "hindered by death" (Hebrews 7:23); one who would be "able to save to the very end those coming through Him to God *because He is* ever living to make intercession for them" (7:25). He would have to be "merciful and faithful" (2:17). He would need to be "pure, innocent, undefiled, separate from the sinners, and become higher than the heavens" themselves (7:26). He would have to bear "no daily need... first to offer up sacrifice for His own sins, then for those of the people" (7:27). Rather, this great High Priest—a son of Adam (Luke 3:38), yet separate from Adam's sin—would need to be able to mediate humanity's offering not over and over again "through *the* blood of goats and calves" (Hebrews 9:12), but through the one-of-a-kind blood that would need to be offered only a single time. God would need to send Israel this perfect priest so that He could uniquely bring the greatest of all substitutionary sacrifices for sin. Only in this way could God's road to reconciliation be paved: with the blood singularly sufficient for paying the whole world's debt—"once," forever, and *"for all"* (9:12).

Is there yet hope of an eternal sacrifice for sins for those who believe? Amen, God's perfect love—and endless atonement—comes.

> "[F]or on this day he will make atonement for you, to cleanse you; from all your sins before ADONAI you will be clean." -Leviticus 16:30

CHAPTER 8

God of Faithfulness

The Good News never gives up on you.

Faulty, frail, imperfect Israel had long been waiting at the foot of God's mountain. There, He brought Heaven to earth in preparation for the journey—and the purpose—of their lives. Through the giving of the commands, the construction of the Tent, and the creation of the priesthood, God introduced His people to the means for the remediation of sin. Not only would it form the foundation for their forgiveness, but the bloody basis for the atonement and reconciliation of the world.

Toward the fulfillment of His now-ancient promise, God had finally prepared Israel to depart from their nearly twelve-month stopover. He reminded the people once again of His faithfulness—that He would remember His covenant with Jacob, Isaac and Abraham; that He would give them the land He pledged to them; and that, even when they would break His covenant, He would never "reject them, nor... loathe them *so as* to finish them *and* to break [His] covenant with them" (Leviticus 26:44). Assured that God would remain ever faithful—faithful even to punish their disobedience—on the twentieth day of the second month of the second year since leaving Egypt (Numbers 10:11), Israel resumed their desert crossing.

Now en route to their covenantal home, the people would soon be facing its inhabitants, to dispossess them from the land. Yet with the relatively brief journey barely underway (cf. Deuteronomy 1:2), tired feet and unsatisfied palates once again proved too arduous. The people wasted no time selfishly complaining of their hardships and, consequently, kindling the anger of God (Numbers 11:1-3, 33-34). It's no wonder, then, that when Moses sent Israel's top men to spy out the promised land, the people responded to news of the current occupants' great size and strength with more blubbering, bawling and grumbling. And as the people rose up in rebellion against Moses, God rose up against the people in return, declaring that for every one of the forty days the men had spent scouting about, all of Israel would now spend a year wandering in the wilderness. For their disobedience and unwillingness to put their trust in God, the entire generation of those who had seen His wonders and deliverance in Egypt[12] would not be permitted to live long enough to receive their inheritance in the land (Numbers 14:28-38). Only their children would enter in.

Led about by their gloomy, God-given guardian Moses, Israel roamed and slowly died off in the deserts and lands of other peoples for four decades. Between avoidances and aggressions with other nations, the people routinely rebelled against God and Moses, suffering the wrathful results of their unreasonable revolts. From their constant moaning about food and water (20:2ff), to their recurrent cries to return to Egypt (21:4ff), to their insurrections against Moses (12:1ff, 16:1ff), to their joining themselves to foreign wives and forbidden gods (25:1ff), Israel would repeatedly antagonize their long-suffering Maker and inflame His jealousy, wrath and judgment.

---

[12] with the exception of faithful Joshua and Caleb

Yet the God of Faithfulness would not merely sow vengeance upon His ungrateful ones, but mercy, should they regret their unfaithful ways. When the people once again spoke against God, loathing His provision and lamenting their freedom, God sent upon them a plague of poisonous snakes, so that as the people were bitten, they would die. But when the people confessed their sins and sought Moses' intercession, God told him to cast a brass serpent and lift it up for all the people to see. So "if the serpent had bitten ANY man, and he looked EXPECTINGLY to the serpent of brass—he lived" (Numbers 21:4-9)...

...just as God would one day lift up another Sign for all to see "so that everyone who is believing in Him may have life everlasting" (John 3:14f).

God did not let His people's wanderings go to waste, for He would use their disloyal defiance to test and perhaps to humble them (Deuteronomy 8:2f). Moses, for his part, would try to keep the peace. He urged ADONAI to remember His promise to not utterly destroy Israel, while exhorting the people to leave behind their headstrong ways. Moses spoke to Israel in covenantal terms, reminding them of their chosenness as the unique people of God (7:6-8). But it would never be enough for them to simply have the defining mark of circumcision in their flesh. To be God's set-apart intermediaries to the world, they needed also to "circumcise the foreskin of [their] heart, and not stiffen [their] neck anymore" (10:16). As it would be also for their descendants, they could not be Israel "*only so* outwardly"— continuing in their self-centered, obstinate ways. They needed also to be God's people inwardly, with a "circumcision... *also of the heart*" (Romans 2:28-29). Nevertheless, Israel remained as stiff-necked and stubborn as ever (Deuteronomy 9:6).

Finally, after four decades of waiting—a whole generation gone—it was time to receive the promise. In Moses' last days, he recounted Israel's history and journey, reminding the remnant of who they were meant to be, and of what they were about to receive. On the edge of destiny, the people stood before God and entered once again into the covenant He had sworn centuries before to the patriarchs (29:9-12[10-13]). For listening *faithfully* to God's voice and being *obedient* to His commands, Moses assured them that God's abundant blessings would come upon them and overtake them (28:2). And for being *unfaithful* to listen to God's voice, and for being *disobedient* to His commands, Moses assured them that abundant curses would come upon them — and pursue them, and overtake them to their destruction (28:45). Then Moses put before them one final, clear and simple choice.

> "See, I have set before you today life and good, and death and evil, in that I am commanding you today to love ADONAI your God, to walk in His ways, and to guard His commands and His statutes and His judgments. And you will live and multiply, and ADONAI your God will bless you in the land where you are going in to possess it. But if your heart turns *away*, and you do not listen... I declare to you this day that you will be certainly destroyed...."
> –Deuteronomy 30:15-18

Moses had been God's hands, feet and voice to Israel for more than forty years. Not only had he led a lost and helpless people out of oppression and bondage, He had established their system of government, instituted their way of life, and interceded with God on their behalf, conveying His commands and cooling His wrath. Moses' value to his people cannot be overstated. The inevitable loss of Moses would be an inestimable loss to the entire Israelite nation.

But lose him they would.

Soon, Moses would be gone—seeing the promised land only from afar—and a new leader would be appointed to complete Israel's covenantal conquest. But because the previous generation had begged God to speak to them only through the mouth of their deliverer, in Moses' absence, God promised to one day "raise up to them a prophet like [Moses] from among their brothers; and [to] put [God's] words in his mouth, and he will speak to them all that which [God would] command him" (18:18). Israel would not hear that Prophet's voice for over a thousand years, and they would succeed and struggle, and surmount and stumble, until He who was "truly the Prophet... [would come] to the world" (John 6:14). When that day came, many in Israel still would not "listen to him"—to the "words which he [spoke] in [God's] Name" (Deuteronomy 18:15&19). Yet tens of thousands of Abraham's progeny would not only hear Him, but follow... and the word of that Prophet would change *everything.*

God chose stubborn, rebellious Israel to carry His word to the world—to mediate between God and man, and to restore the created ones to their Creator. Remaining true to His covenant, "the faithful God" (7:9) would bring Israel triumphantly into their homeland, and the inheritance promised to their fathers would finally be granted. The God of Faithfulness—the Bringer of wondrous deliverance, the Giver of holy commands, the Maker of everlasting atonement—chose and then worked through Israel, knowing full well that they would continually let Him down (31:21). But what better way to prove to the world God's unmatched character than to remain *faithful to a broken people* who would so often—and so easily—*break faith* with Him?

The peculiar people of Israel would soon come to despise God and break His covenant (31:20). They would enter into the land which He had faithfully given, and—envying the nations—reject His majesty...

...rejected for an earthly king.

> "I AM ADONAI, your Holy One, Creator of Israel, your King."
> –Isaiah 43:15

CHAPTER 9

God of Redemption

The Good News humbles disobedience, and forgives.

Following the death of Moses, it would be his successor Joshua who would finally bring Israel into the land. With the tablets of the testimony before them, the people set off on their divinely appointed campaign to conquer and resettle their ancestral home. Through obedience to God, miraculously falling walls (Joshua 6:12ff), physics-defying celestial events (10:12f) and over five years of fighting,[13] the land promised to Israel's fathers was theirs... mostly. God had dispossessed the previous occupants because of their wickedness, giving the land to His covenantal people (Deuteronomy 9:4-6, cf. Leviticus 18:3ff). And Israel served ADONAI for all of Joshua's days, and for all the days of the elders who outlived him...

> "[But] another generation arose after them who... did evil in the eyes of ADONAI...." –Judges 2:10-11

Having disobeyed God by not completely driving out the land's inhabitants, Israel activated ADONAI's promise to make

---

[13] It may have taken as many as seven years for the land to be sufficiently conquered (Joshua 14:10), though not completely. Israel would gradually continue taking territory during the ensuing years (Exodus 23:29-30, Joshua 13:1ff).

the remaining nations a thorn in their side (2:3).[14] The foreign religions of those people would become an alluring snare, as Israel continually and repeatedly failed God's test by fervently going after other gods and worshipping them. So for their blatant defiance and grave unfaithfulness, God gave Israel over into the hands of their plunderers. No longer could the sons of Abraham, Isaac and Jacob stand against and conquer their God-strengthened foes (2:14, 3:12). Over the next 300 years, in a recurring cycle of reprieve and defeat, whenever Israel would cry out to God, He would feel sorry for His people — despite their disloyalty — and in His compassion, raise up judges to lead and to save them. Anytime a judge was raised up, God would be with him, and Israel would be delivered. But whenever that judge died, the people "turned back [to other gods] and did more corruptly than their fathers.... They had not fallen *away* from their [evil] practices or from their stiff-*necked* way" (2:19).

> "In those days, there was no king in Israel. Each man did that which was right in his own eyes." -Judges 17:6

As the time of the judges neared its end, God raised up the prophet-priest Samuel—an enduringly upright servant of God, who led his people in righteousness. When Samuel grew old, he made his sons judges over Israel, yet they did not walk in their father's ways, and turned aside after their own gain. Seeing this, the people confronted Samuel and rebuffed the leadership of his rebellious sons. And Israel, seizing the opportunity to object to the status quo and to pursue the ways of the nations (1 Samuel 8:5), demanded for themselves... a king.

---

[14] cf. Numbers 33:55

Aggrieved by their worldly petition, Samuel nevertheless brought the matter before God. And God's reply — to do exactly as the people had said — must have wounded Samuel all the more. Though Samuel warned them of the contempt and harshness they would receive from their requested king (8:11ff), they refused to listen, wanting nothing less than to be led about and lorded over just like the surrounding nations. As God had told Samuel, no longer would the people willingly subject themselves to His reign:

> "Listen to the voice of the people, to all that they say to you, for they have not rejected you; rather, they have rejected Me...." –1 Samuel 8:7

So God sent Saul to be king over Israel, and in him, the people received the king they deserved.

An oppressive ruler, Saul would force the people into his personal service and make them work his land. Having come from wealth and privilege, he would take the people's choice harvests for his own, and the whole nation would become as fearful slaves (8:11-18). But what the people had most desired was a warrior king who would handily defeat their enemies. And despite the harsh conditions with which Saul afflicted Israel, in war, at least, he delivered. Wherever Saul turned, he crushed Israel's foes. Yet the greatest casualty of the wars of Saul would not be left on the battlefield. For all of his success in warfare, Saul nevertheless foolishly engaged in armed conflict with God.

Saul repeatedly skirted the instructions of his Commander, feigning compliance while making excuses for his circumventions. Even in the offering of sacrifices meant for pleasing God, in reality, Saul only sought what pleased himself, shortcutting

ADONAI's commands as he wished. Saul desired spectacle and attention over humility and obedience, believing in his arrogant pride that he knew better than God. It was therefore in the face of this fatal flaw that Samuel announced the king of Israel's inevitable—and more excellent—replacement.

> "You [Saul] have not guarded the command of ADONAI your God... for then ADONAI would have established your kingdom over Israel forever. But now your kingdom will not stand. ADONAI has sought for Himself a man according to His own heart, and ADONAI gives charge to him as leader over His people...." –1 Samuel 13:13-14

Like the ungrateful assembly who demanded a king, Saul had turned away from God and rejected Him. By putting his personal concerns above ADONAI's commands, Saul became the cause of his own eventual downfall. The line of his kingship would soon abruptly end.

A new king—a humble king—was coming. The God of Redemption was about to give Israel—and everyone, everywhere—the King they *didn't* deserve.

Endless Kingdom, Eternal Throne

Rejected by both His people and their king, God nevertheless remained faithful to His covenant and to His plan of reconciliation and salvation for the world. Despite the people's treasonous intentions in demanding a king, God would redeem their evil plea by establishing a king in Israel with a heart both for righteousness and for Him. From the sons of a lowly shepherd, ADONAI would choose His true champion. To correct the people's mistake in King Saul, the God of Redemption would restore Israel's kingdom in David.

Directed by God, Samuel found and privately anointed young David well over a decade before he would ascend to the throne (16:13). Saul, in need of a musician, soon brought David into his service, and also chose him as his armor-bearer (16:21). Eventually, David earned his place as a warrior in the king's army, having had great success in battle and giant-slaying (18:5). Though Saul greatly loved David (16:21), finding relief in the anointed musician's hands, he began to feel threatened as David surpassed him in winning the love and adoration of all the people. Before long, Saul grew to fully fear him, "for ADONAI had been with [David], and from Saul He had turned aside" (18:12ff).

As the Spirit of ADONAI departed from Saul in exchange for a torturous spirit from God (18:10), his mind darkened, and he grew increasingly obsessed with the unassuming shepherd's son. The more success and love that David obtained, the more paranoid Saul became. Soon he devolved into a spear-throwing, scheming, vindictive shell of a king, and so "Saul was an enemy to David all the days" (18:29).

With a kill order issued to his servants, and even a direct assassination attempt or two of his own, Saul's fixation on the future king sent David running for his life (19:1). Chased by Saul's men, going from city to city, evading capture and living in caves, the man of God still managed to maintain both his integrity and his sanity. Without malice or hatred for his king, David would forfeit multiple opportunities to slay his pursuer and end his persecution (24:4[3]ff, 26:11ff). But even when David offered undeniable proof of his boundless loyalty, Saul could only see his usurper.

And, after forty grueling years as king of Israel, Saul unceremoniously fell in battle, never having dispatched his imagined nemesis.

Mourning the passing of Saul, David finally returned from exile, with his great exploits of years past still fresh in the minds of the people. David was immediately made king over his birth-tribe of Judah (2 Samuel 2:4), and after seven years of further infighting and adversity, at long last, the humble king took his place on Israel's throne (5:3).

> "...and David went on, going on and becoming great, and ADONAI... WAS with him." –2 Samuel 5:10

When David had finally been given rest from all his enemies, he became deeply moved concerning the Creator's temporary Tent among His people, and desired in his heart to build for Him a permanent home (7:1-3). Seeing David's devotion to bless Him with a Temple, which He had never asked for nor commanded, ADONAI responded not simply with affirmation, but with a promise to build the house of David instead. The God of Redemption covenanted with David[15] that of his descendants who would sit on Israel's throne, there would be no end.

> "And ADONAI has declared to you [David] that ADONAI will make a house for you.... I will raise up your [son] after you.... He will build a house [Temple] for My Name,[16] and I will establish the throne of his kingdom forever.... And your house and your kingdom will be made steadfast before your face forever; your throne will be established forever." –2 Samuel 7:11c-16

---

[15] cf. Psalm 89:3, 2 Chronicles 7:18

[16] Though God approved of David himself, David's experiences as a warrior nevertheless disqualified him from building the Temple (see 1 Chronicles 22:8). David's son Solomon would complete its construction.

Upon the heart of David — the man after God's own heart — ADONAI would establish his eternal throne. David had done nothing to earn such unconditional commitment from Israel's God except to exceed all others in humility and love. Though David would now serve Israel as the template of a good and righteous king, he still would not escape his own adulterous and murderous moral failures (11:1ff) and the agonizing consequences that would result (12:14). But because of his repentant heart before God, the turmoil he continued to endure, and the forgiveness and restoration he would faithfully receive (12:24), David could fathom—perhaps better than most—the lengths and depths of the God of Redemption...

...who shelters the soul of the outcast (Psalm 71:23)...

...who raises up life from the pit (Psalm 103:4)...

...who ties His reputation to the restoration of His one-of-a-kind people (2 Samuel 7:23)...

...who is ever-willing to redeem His covenant with Israel (Psalm 111:5-9).

For forty years, David reigned as king. Yet after his death, in just forty years more, the kingdom would split itself in two (1 Kings 11:42-12:19). Though David's eternal line would eventually appear to reach its end, still, the guarantee and hope of God's covenant would endure. From that broken line, ADONAI would one day raise up David's greatest Son to sit forever upon his throne. That King of all kings would be not just the redeemer of Israel, but the One to offer redemption to every living soul.

The God of David was still making a Way to accept those who didn't deserve to be accepted. Through Israel's humble king, the God of Redemption showed His willingness to redeem even those who appear irredeemable.

> "Blessed IS ADONAI, the God of Israel, Because He looked upon *us*, And worked redemption for His people, And raised a horn of salvation to us, In the house of David His servant..." –Luke 1:68-69

CHAPTER 10

God of Revelation

The Good News reveals the end from the beginning.

Over the course of nearly half a millennium, the kings and kingdoms of Israel underwent sweeping and turbulent change. As promised, God had indeed built the house of the quintessential king David, establishing his throne through David's specially selected son, Solomon. Blessed with great wisdom and riches, Solomon fulfilled God's word to David and succeeded in constructing the holy Temple of ADONAI. But though Solomon had followed God as a faithful son for most of his days, when he was old, he faltered and turned to other gods. It was a state of disobedience that would come with kingdom-sized consequences (1 Kings 11:11ff).

Upon Solomon's death, God executed His judgment, and the vast majority of the people of Israel rejected Solomon's foolish successor (1 Kings 12:1ff). They broke away from the tribe of Judah and the chosen line of kings, proceeding to set up their own ruler and to form a new, separate kingdom of Israel. The people of this northern dominion were plagued by their own continual sin as they abandoned all the commands of ADONAI, forged idols and images, sacrificed their children, and worshiped and served false gods (2 Kings 17:16ff). And within two and half centuries, they had met their ultimate end, having been completely conquered—carried off and scattered by a brutal and powerful foreign regime.

Meanwhile, the much smaller southern kingdom of Judah failed to fare much better. In a recurring cycle between obedience to God and rebellion against His commands, Judah was constantly waxing between prosperity and foreign subjection, as God would cause her good kings to rise and her evil ones to fall. Judah would ultimately come to emulate and embrace northern Israel's sinful customs, and, following the death of Judah's last righteous king, the kingdom would enter into its most rapid decline. Invading forces soon destroyed the city of Jerusalem and the holy Temple, and forcibly removed the remnant of the Jewish people from their promised land (24:20ff). In little more than a century after the dispersion of the north, Judah was also taken into captivity by an alien, conquering nation.

Yet even while God's covenantal people were managing to almost completely forsake their set-apart purpose, the voice of the God of Revelation had not been silent. In the midst of such grave disobedience and completely avoidable upheaval, God continually raised up admonishing prophets, not only to warn His people to return to Him, but also to foretell the restoration of the kingdom—indeed, of the entire world—through Israel's last hope and eternal King...

... the coming Son of David, the one and only Messiah.

As it is written in the prophets, this Messiah's origins would be "of old"—His beginnings from "the days of antiquity" (Micah 5:1[2]).[17] ADONAI would raise Him up from among His people

---

[17] Fulfilled prophecy according to John 1:1-2,18, 8:58, Ephesians 1:3-4, Colossians 1:15-19 and Revelation 1:18.

Israel as "a prophet like [Moses]," putting His own words into his mouth so that his brothers might hear and heed (Deuteronomy 18:15-19).[18] He would make atonement once and for all, as "a priest forever" in an eternal and perfect priestly order (Psalm 110:4).[19] His "scepter will not turn aside from Judah" (Genesis 49:10), for He will be the everlasting King of the Jews.[20]

This Messiah would come from the line of David—a "righteous sprout" raised up to him (Jeremiah 23:5); a fruitful "shoot... from the stem of" his father (Isaiah 11:1,10). He would *"reign* on the throne of David and over his kingdom" for the rest of time (Isaiah 9:6[7]),[21] and, like David before Him, ADONAI would declare Him to be "My son" (Psalm 2:7).[22] The Spirit of ADONAI would rest upon him (Isaiah 11:2), because ADONAI would anoint Him "to proclaim good news to the afflicted" (Isaiah 61:1).[23] He would be called "God" (Psalm 45:6) and bear the Name of "ADONAI our righteousness" (Jeremiah 23:6). "He will call his name Wonderful, Counselor, Mighty God, Father of Eternity, Prince of Peace" (Isaiah 9:5[6]).[24]

This Messiah would be born in the Judean city of Bethlehem (Micah 5:1[2]), and live by Israel's Sea of the Galilee (Isaiah 8:23

---

[18] Fulfilled, Acts 3:20-22 and 7:37.

[19] Fulfilled, Hebrews 5:6, 6:20, 7:15-17.

[20] Fulfilled, Matthew 2:2, 27:29; Mark 15:2, 15:26; Luke 23:38; John 19:19.

[21] Fulfilled, Matthew 1:1,6; Acts 13:22-23; Romans 1:3, 15:12; Revelation 5:5, 22:16; cf. Hebrews 1:8

[22] Fulfilled, Acts 13:32-33; Hebrews 1:5, 5:5-6.

[23] Fulfilled, Matthew 3:16; John 1:32-33, 3:34; Luke 4:17-21; Acts 10:38.

[24] Fulfilled, John 1:1-2, 10:30; Philippians 2:9-11; 1 Corinthians 1:30, Hebrews 1:8.

[9:1]f).²⁵ The sign of His birth would be His pregnant virgin mother (Isaiah 7:14),²⁶ with the exact timing of His arrival perhaps forecasted in advance (Daniel 9:24-26). He would be heralded by a messenger, preparing "the way of ADONAI" for Him in the Israeli deserts (Isaiah 40:3, Malachi 3:1).²⁷ He would open blind eyes and unstop deaf ears (Isaiah 35:5-6); He would carry our sicknesses (53:4),²⁸ proclaiming the salvation and liberty that can set everyone free (61:1).²⁹

This Messiah—Israel's King—would enter Jerusalem in lowliness and humility (Zechariah 9:9).³⁰ Yet He would be "despised and rejected" (Isaiah 53:3, Psalm 118:22)³¹ by those gathered against Him—"against ADONAI and against His Messiah" (Psalm 2:1-2).³² Upon Him would fall the disgraces of those who would resist and condemn and denounce Him (69:10[9]).³³ His lying enemies would be abundant and powerful—each of them "hating [Him] without cause" (35:19, 69:4).³⁴

And as it is written in the prophets, this Messiah would be betrayed by a close companion, one with whom He would break

---

²⁵ Fulfilled, Matthew 2:1, 4:12-16; Luke 2:4-7; John 7:42.

²⁶ Fulfilled, Matthew 1:18-2:1, Luke 1:26-35.

²⁷ Fulfilled, Matthew 11:10, Luke 1:17.

²⁸ Fulfilled, Matthew 8:17, 11:5; John 5:8.

²⁹ Fulfilled, Luke 4:17-21.

³⁰ Fulfilled, Matthew 21:1-11, Mark 11:1-11.

³¹ Fulfilled, John 1:11; Luke 9:22, 17:25; Acts 4:11.

³² Fulfilled, Acts 4:25-27.

³³ Fulfilled, Romans 15:3.

³⁴ Fulfilled, John 15:25.

bread (41:10[9]).³⁵ Those nearest to Him would desert Him in His greatest hour of need, like a scattered flock whose shepherd had been stricken (Zechariah 13:7).³⁶ He would be oppressed and afflicted by those judging Him, yet answer the accusations against Him with silence (Isaiah 53:7-8).³⁷ And though He would have "done no wrong" (53:9),³⁸ with no deceit found in His mouth (53:9), He would be convicted with—and stand counted among—the worst of sinners (53:12).³⁹

This Messiah would be repeatedly struck and spat upon (50:6)⁴⁰—His body pierced at his hands and feet and side (Psalm 22:17[16], Zechariah 12:10).⁴¹ In the midst of His distress, He would be scorned and despised—insulted and mocked for His ability to save (Psalm 22:8[7]f).⁴² Those who mercilessly scourged Him would "cast lots for [His] clothing" (22:19[18]),⁴³ and provide only vinegar-wine for His thirst (22:16[15], 69:22[21]).⁴⁴ Yet despite the excruciating agony, "not one of [His bones would be] broken"

---

[35] Fulfilled, Matthew 10:4, 26:50; John 13:18-27.

[36] Fulfilled, Matthew 26:31, 56.

[37] Fulfilled, Matthew 26:63, 27:12-14; 1 Peter 2:23; Acts 8:32-33.

[38] Fulfilled, 1 Peter 2:22.

[39] Fulfilled, Matthew 27:38, Luke 22:37.

[40] Fulfilled, Matthew 26:67, 27:30; Luke 22:63f; John 18:22.

[41] Fulfilled, Matthew 27:35; Mark 15:24; Luke 24:39; John 19:18, 34, 37, 20:20-28; Revelation 1:7.

[42] Fulfilled, Matthew 27:31-44, Luke 23:35-39.

[43] Fulfilled, Matthew 27:35, Mark 15:24, Luke 23:34, John 19:24.

[44] Fulfilled, Matthew 27:48, Mark 15:36, Luke 23:36, John 19:28-30.

(Psalm 34:21[20], cf. Exodus 12:46),[45] and in His death, He would be laid to rest in a rich man's grave (Isaiah 53:9).[46]

Then the Creator of the Universe would raise up this Messiah from the dead (Psalm 16:10),[47] and with Him would come Israel's salvation (Isaiah 49:5) — and the salvation of everyone (49:6) — from their sin:[48]

> And he was pierced for our violations,
> Crushed for our *causes of* guilt,
> The chastisement for our peace IS on him,
> And by his wound there is healing to us.
> All of us like sheep have gone astray,
> Each to his own way we have turned,
> And ADONAI has laid upon him
> The guilt of us all.
> He had been oppressed and afflicted,
> And he opened not his mouth;
> As a lamb to the slaughter he was brought....
> And ADONAI had delighted to crush him.[49]
> He had made him sick.
> If his soul will make a guilt offering,
> He will see *his* seed—he will prolong *his* days,
> And the pleasure of ADONAI will prosper in his hand.

---

[45] Fulfilled, John 19:33-36.

[46] Fulfilled, Matthew 27:57-60, Mark 15:43-46, Luke 23:50-53, John 19:38-42.

[47] Fulfilled, Matthew 28:1-20; Acts 2:23-36, 3:15, 13:33-37; 1 Corinthians 15:4-6.

[48] Fulfilled, Mark 10:45; John 1:29, 3:16; Acts 8:30-35.

[49] cf. Psalm 22:1, Matthew 27:46, Mark 15:34.

> From the suffering of his soul he will see—he will be satisfied.
> Through his knowledge, the righteous one—My servant—
> Will give righteousness to many,
> And their *causes of* guilt he will bear.
>
> –Isaiah 53:5-7, 10-11

So it is written in the prophets.

After seventy years, Judah completed her allotted time of punishment in exile, and God released Israel's Jewish remnant from captivity (Jeremiah 25:11, 29:10). A conquered and defeated people, they slowly returned to the Land, though they would continue to live under foreign influence and rule. Despite the occasional repentance and revolt, Israel remained in a compromised state of assimilation for more than half a millennium. And though the prophetic voice of God would continue to speak for a little while, the legitimate throne of David remained woefully unoccupied.

Since the time of Adam—for four thousand years—mankind had remained separate from and unreconciled to God. Though He had prepared a succession of redemptive doorways through which man might walk, a sin-stained return proved impossible. But in the fullness of time, the God of Revelation would reveal the narrow door of salvation—the culmination of all that had come before. God would finally show Israel—and the whole world—The Way...

CHAPTER 11

God of Love

The Good News gives until there is nothing left to give.

At long last, the people of Israel had returned to their homeland, now a broken and castaway nation. Though they managed to rebuild both Jerusalem and the House of God, they nevertheless remained under the thumb of external subjugation, governed by a succession of warring, foreign empires. Under the influence of their ungodly occupiers, many of the people held onto and adopted foreign customs alien to the will and word of God. They spawned the corruption of their own priesthood,[50] endured the installation of puppet kings, and formed competing segments of a new, Temple-less Jewish religion—a religion that had been imported from their excursion into exile.[51] The kingdom of Israel—the nation of God's covenant people—was barely more than an empty shell.

---

[50] The hellenization of Israel and degraded status of the priesthood is documented in Jewish writings from the intertestamental period, including the accounts of the Maccabees.

[51] This "Temple-less" religion revolved around the synagogue, as it still does today. "The synagogue as a permanent institution originated probably in the period of the Babylonian captivity, when a place for common worship and instruction had become necessary." Bacher, Wilhelm and Dembitz, Lewis N. "Synagogue." *The Jewish Encyclopedia*, New York and London: Funk & Wagnalls Company, 1906.

> "But when the fullness of time came, God sent forth His Son (having come from a woman)..." -Galatians 4:4

With echoes of an ancient past, God once again placed His people's future in the lap of obscurity. In one of Israel's unremarkable towns, God chose for Himself an unremarkable man... one who just happened to be the descendant of the kind of men that patriarchs and kings *and saviors* are made of. But when this insignificant carpenter found His virgin betrothed-one with child, it would take an angelic appearance to convince Him of what the *God of Creation* was about to do. The Word of God, through whom everyone and everything had been made since the beginning, would now Himself miraculously become... *a human being* (John 1:1-3,14).

He would be a son of Adam, a son of Abraham, and a son of David (Matthew 1:1). This great "Son of the Highest" would ascend to "the throne of David His father," and through Him, the *God of Redemption* would restore that failed and broken covenantal line. As the eternal King of the Jews, He would "reign over the house of Jacob to the ages," and of His awesome and everlasting reign "there will be no end" (Luke 1:32-33). This is the One whom Israel had been waiting for: a King, "a Savior—who is Messiah, the Master" (Luke 2:11). And because this One would not simply save His people, but "save [them] from their sins" (Matthew 1:21), His Name would be called...

...Yeshua.[52]

For His first three decades, Israel's humble King would live the normal, unassuming life of a Jewish tradesman's son. He was circumcised on the eighth day according to the covenant

---

[52] "Yeshua" in Hebrew—יְשׁוּעַ!—literally means "salvation" (יְשׁוּעָה).

of the Torah (Luke 2:21), given the redemption of the firstborn at the Temple (2:22ff), and lived in obedient submission to His dutiful and faithful parents (2:51). As Yeshua grew, the young man continued to advance in wisdom and stature. Israel's hidden Messiah would find favor both with God and with men (2:52).

When He was about thirty years old, Yeshua seemingly burst onto the public scene. He began to proclaim a message to the people of Israel concerning some kind of "Good News," saying that the Kingdom of God was at hand, but that they must repent of their ungodly ways (Mark 1:15) and be spiritually born again (John 3:3ff). Everywhere He traveled, He declared liberty from a bondage that many didn't even know they had—teaching that everyone who sins is a slave to it, but that the truth of His word would make them free (8:32ff). Reports of this powerful new voice quickly spread throughout the surrounding region, as He spoke also at the Temple and in the synagogues. As He stood up to read on one particular Shabbat,[53] having unrolled the scroll of the prophet Isaiah, He read aloud,

> "The Spirit of ADONAI is upon me,
> Because He anointed me
> To proclaim Good News to the poor;
> Sent me to proclaim release to captives,
> And receiving of sight to the blind;
> To send out the bruised with release;
> To proclaim the acceptable year of ADONAI."
> –Luke 4:18-19 (cf. Isaiah 61:1-2)

"And having folded the scroll, having given IT back to the attendant, He sat down.... And He began to say to them, 'Today this Scripture has been fulfilled in your ears.' And all... were

---

[53] "Shabbat" or "Sabbath"

in wonder at the favorable words that were coming out of His mouth" (Luke 4:20-22). And from that moment, the *God of Revelation* began to make His plans clear. Everything written about the Messiah in the Torah, the Prophets and the Psalms was finally about to be fully revealed.

Teacher of Israel

Yeshua would travel all across the Land of Israel proclaiming this Good News, gathering disciples to His revolutionary cause and displaying unusual feats of supernatural power never before seen on Earth. His closest friends would witness Him turn water into wine (John 2:6ff), calm storms with His words (Mark 4:36ff), and walk unwaveringly on deep, turbulent water as if upon dry ground (Matthew 14:25ff). Among His throngs of followers, He would miraculously heal the afflicted of their disease, cure the crippled of their infirmity, and give once-blind eyes the ability to see (John 9:25). And everywhere that He walked, and talked, and healed, and wept, and confronted, and pursued, and provoked, He would compellingly—and divinely—expound the word of God.

The Master Yeshua exalted and upheld the Torah, declaring that for all time not even its tiniest letter would fall or pass away (Matthew 5:17, Luke 16:17). He affirmed how Moses taught obedience to the *God of Commandments* as a function of true love, citing the summary directives to be wholly devoted to Him, and to lovingly treat our neighbors as ourselves (Matthew 22:37ff, Mark 12:28ff, Luke 10:25ff). Yeshua proclaimed how the first Hebrew patriarch—who, at God's word, was willing to put the life of his son at stake—had gazed through time and space to see the Creator of the Universe offer up His own (John 8:56ff). He professed how the *God of Promise* would ultimately bring His people into an undying land, where our Father Abraham is alive and well, and where those who believe in Yeshua will also live forever (Matthew 22:31f, Luke 20:37f). He taught how the *God of Judgment* would give eternal life to the righteous, but everlasting punishment to the wicked (Matthew 25:33ff). And Yeshua pointed to Himself as the living bread from Heaven (John 6:51), the light of the world (9:5), and the perfect rescue vessel from sin and death. He alone would be the last escape route long envisioned by the *God of Salvation:* the difficult road, the narrow door, the way, the truth, and the life (Matthew 7:13f; Luke 13:24; John 10:1ff, 14:6).

God sent Yeshua "to the lost sheep of the house of Israel" (Matthew 15:24) to bring to His people the knowledge of this salvation from sin. He offered such forgiveness explicitly to His fellow Jews so that God might declare them righteous and fit to fulfill their covenantal, restorative role to the world (as Yeshua declared in John 4:22, "salvation is of the Jews"). Yet forgiveness could not come without a price. The costliness of sin would require far more than words.

And the God of Love was prepared to pay it... with the life of His only Son.

> "In this is the love: not that we loved God, but that He loved us, and sent His Son as an appeasement for our sins." -1 John 4:10

For three years, Yeshua continued His itinerant instruction and spiritual shepherding all throughout Roman-occupied Israel. As news of Him reached every corner of the Land, thousands of Jews would flock to hear His words and wisdom, as well as to receive both healing for their sicknesses and hope for themselves, their people, and the future. This astonishing teacher was proclaiming a message of life and deliverance, explaining to them with an authority that surpassed even that of the religious leaders. The people began to fill with anticipation that the Prophet promised by Moses had finally come to them (John 7:40).[54] Many even professed that Yeshua was the Anointed One, the long-awaited Son of David (7:41). And many more dared to whisper—and then to cry aloud—that this Prophet... this Messiah... was Israel's true and coming King.

With the masses enthralled by this ever-rising voice within Israel, Yeshua's growing popularity quickly caught the attention of the skeptics—not to mention Israel's religious elite. Yeshua often found Himself locked in theological debate with the clerics and scribes, confronting their customs and beliefs, and challenging them to return to the word of God as encoded in Israel's sacred Scriptures. Yeshua's call to national repentance and expectation of a new Kingdom was perceived by some as a threat—in part to the status quo of foreign occupation, but more to the power of Jewish civic and religious leadership. And His unusual, often inflammatory rhetoric did nothing to calm such concerns, but rather delineated a bright line for the people of Israel: whether they would accept or reject God's ultimate salvation.

Weaved throughout His speaking, Yeshua began to assert a unique relationship with the one He called "the Father"—His reference to God. He said the most curious things, such as, "he who is not honoring the Son does not honor the Father who sent him" (5:23) and "no one comes to the Father unless through Me" (14:6) and "I and the Father are one" (10:30). On very few occasions, He was even somewhat less cryptic, going so far as to utter the shocking claim that He was, in fact, God's own Son

---

[54] Deuteronomy 18:15; Acts 3:22, 7:37

(10:36). Yeshua had already been stirring things up through His frequent conflicts with leadership and very public breaking of tradition, inciting an increasing number within Israel to persecute Him and seek His death. So when the crowds heard Him essentially "calling God His own Father, making Himself equal to God," they were looking to kill Him all the more (5:18).

It would not be long before the plot to eliminate Yeshua would be executed.

A New Covenant

When the day for the annual Passover feast had arrived, Yeshua knew that His time was near (Matthew 26:18). Desiring to share His final Passover with His closest disciples, He sent them on ahead to prepare the foretelling meal.

That evening, as they remembered the ancient enslavement of their people and the mighty hand of God's historic salvation, Yeshua took the unleavened bread, broke it, and distributed it among His disciples. Recalling the slaughter of those first Passover sacrifices 1500 years earlier, He said of the broken, symbolic bread, "This is My body that is being given for you; do this to *the* remembrance of Me" (Luke 22:19). And in recognition of the lambs' innocent blood—the blood that had been applied to the doorposts of Israel's homes; the blood that had set God's people free from Egyptian slavery and death—He took the fruit of the vine and gave it to them, saying, "This cup *is* the new covenant in My blood that is being poured out for you... for release from sins" (Luke 22:20, Matthew 26:28).

By the sinless, battered body and guiltless blood of "the Lamb of God, who is taking away the sin of the world" (John 1:29), Yeshua would soon complete the story of Israel's exodus. The doorposts of their *hearts* could now be painted, and the houses of their *bodies* passed over by Death. Just as God had sent a deliverer to save Israel from slavery in Egypt, now the Jewish people were about to receive *eternal* deliverance from their enslavement to sin. They would be brought by a mighty hand and an outstretched arm into the *everlasting* promised Land.

Through the Messiah's Passover sacrifice, not only would the *God of Faithfulness* keep His covenants with Israel, but the God of Love—fulfilling the word of the prophet—would make with them a *new* one.

> "Look! days are coming"—an utterance of ADONAI—
> "That I will make with the house of Israel
> And with the house of Judah a new covenant,
> Not like the covenant I made with their fathers
> (In the day of My taking their hand
> To bring them out of the land of Egypt),
> In that they broke My covenant,
> Though I ruled over them....
> For this *is* the covenant that I will make
> With the house of Israel after those days:
> ...I will put My Torah in their inward part,
> And I will write it on their heart,
> And I will be to them for *their* God,
> And they will be to Me for *My* people.
> And they will no longer teach
> Each *one* his neighbor and each *one* his brother
> Saying, 'Know ADONAI,'
> For they will all know Me, from their least to their greatest...
> For I will forgive their guilt,
> And of their sin I will make remembrance no more."
> —Jeremiah 31:31-34

God's New Covenant with Israel—established in Yeshua's body; ratified by His blood—would restore His covenantal relationship with His people. Because they had forsaken the Torah and broken the covenant of their fathers, Yeshua was sent to be the "mediator of a better covenant... sanctioned *by Torah* on better promises" (Hebrews 8:6). Through Yeshua, the reconciliation between God and man would no longer depend on a temporary atonement from the blood of goats or bulls. Rather, by the Messiah's very own blood, mankind would soon find the permanent path to the forgiveness of their guilt—and the way would be made for God to forget all of our sins forever.

After the meal and into the night, Yeshua retreated with His disciples to pray in a secluded place outside Jerusalem. Heavy-hearted and exceedingly sorrowful in His soul, He cried out to the Father, seeking God's divine intervention and will (Matthew 26:37ff). As He rose from His prayers and woke His sleeping disciples, He found a swiftly approaching armed mob which had been assembled by Israel's hardened conspirators. And with the enlistment of a traitor and the muscle of the Roman government, the Jewish authorities secured Yeshua's arrest, His disciples scattered, and His appointed fate was sealed (Mark 14:43ff, John 18:3).

In covetous fear, the high priest and the entire Jewish council sought the death penalty for their Savior (Mark 14:55). To justify such a sentence, they proceeded to conduct a sham trial complete with a parade of false, unreliable witnesses. Yet, despite their best efforts, they were easily frustrated, being unable to corroborate the conflicting testimony (14:56). Finally, in utter exasperation, the high priest rose up among them and, questioning Yeshua directly, asked Him, "Are you the Messiah—the Son of the Blessed *One*?" (14:61). And Yeshua—admitting the truth, claiming to be the Son of God, and thereby assuring His own conviction—confessed to His singular, undeniable offense: "I am" (14:62). That was all they needed to hear. There was no need for further witnesses. The high priest tore his clothes and pronounced the crime of blasphemy, and then they each declared Yeshua "worthy of death" (14:64). The ones holding Him spat in His face; they blindfolded Him, they slapped Him, and they beat Him. And by morning, the matter was settled...

The leadership of Israel was ready to hand over their one, true Messiah to be crucified.

What Love Was Prepared to Pay

Determined to have Yeshua put to death, the Jewish council dragged Him before the Roman governor of Judea. In an attempt to draw Rome into their plot, they listed their accusations and false charges, imploring the governor to carry out their desired sentence (Luke 23:2, John 18:31). Initially dismissive, the governor eventually questioned Yeshua concerning the allegation of His claim to be king of the Jews. Yet despite His profession that He was indeed "born, and... come to the world [to be king, so that He] may testify to the truth" (John 18:37), the governor found no fault with Him, and decided to let Him go. The council, however, was insistent and pushed back on the decision, keeping the proceedings alive.

So Yeshua was sent before the tetrarch of Galilee...

No fault found.

He was returned to the Roman governor...

No fault found.

Nothing done by Yeshua—or claimed to have been done by Him—was determined by any other authority to be worthy of capital punishment. But the leaders of Israel, refusing to accept the verdict, proceeded to incite a riot among the people and force the governor's hand (Mark 15:11, Matthew 27:24).

"What evil did he do?"

"Crucify him!"

"I find no cause for death in him."

"Crucify, crucify him!"

And "they were pressing *him* with loud voices, asking *for* [Yeshua] to be crucified, and their voices were prevailing" (Luke 23:21-23). So to pacify the crowd, the governor whipped and tore the flesh of the Savior of the world, and then immediately sentenced Him to death.

The battalion of Roman soldiers gathered together and surrounded Him... humiliating, abusing, tormenting. After stripping Him naked, they draped Him in imitative royal garb. They gave Him a reed for a scepter and thorns for a crown, and then knelt mockingly before the One at whose Name every knee will one day bow (Philippians 2:10). They hurled insults, spat on Him, and struck Him violently and repeatedly on His head and face. And when they were finished with their torturous taunting, they led Yeshua away to crucify Him (Matthew 27:28ff).

Upon His back, as He carried the stake for His own execution (John 19:17), Yeshua bore the unbearable weight not only of the whole world's sins, but also of Israel's covenants, patriarchs and promises. The culmination of all that God had been working to restore since the beginning rested literally on the Messiah's beaten and bloody shoulders. Like a sheep led to the slaughter, Yeshua silently slogged His way to the site of His slow assassination. But what the fearful and jealous ones of Israel had devised for evil, the *God of Deliverance* had devised for good... and the willing sacrifice of the innocent Lamb of God was about to repair the world.

It would be no quick death upon an altar of bronze and wood. Instead they hung Him there, upright, His arms and feet impaled against the thick crossbeam and post. The suffocating force of gravity pushed down relentlessly on His shredded and exhausted body—flesh-ripping with every inhalation, asphyxiating with each release. Suspended there in anguish — hour upon hour, mangled and suffering — He could hear only the scoffing and ridicule of those He was sent to serve. "He has trusted on God — LET HIM NOW DELIVER HIM..." "He saved others, *but* he is not able to save himself!" "The Messiah! The king of Israel! Let him come down now from the stake, so that we may see and believe" (Matthew 27:43, Mark 15:31f). But only creation replied — as if in anguish itself — shrouding the daylight and sending darkness throughout the land (Matthew 27:45).

A shaking, withering silhouette—burning from crippling agony and thirst — Yeshua was suddenly overcome with a spark of strength. Mustering every ounce He had, the Son of David shouted in a loud, silence-shattering voice, "MY GOD! MY GOD! WHY DID YOU ABANDON ME?" (Matthew 27:46). An excruciating cry from an ancient past, the intense and timeless echoes of Israel's King rang out.

> My God, my God, why have You forsaken me?
> *Why are You* far from my salvation *and* the words of my groaning?...

> All *those who are* seeing me mock me,
> They make free with the lip *and* shake the head, *saying*,
> "Trust on ADONAI; let Him rescue him.
> He will deliver him, for He has delighted in him...."
> My power is dried up as pottery,
> And my tongue is sticking to my jaws.
> And you appoint me to the dust of death.
> For dogs have surrounded me,
> A community of evil doers have encompassed me,
> Piercing[55] my hands and my feet.
> –Psalm 22:2,8-9,16-17[1,7-8,15-16]

And as Yeshua shouted again with a loud, thunderous voice, the rift of thousands of years — the distance and separation and estrangement and antagonism and grief and regret and division — between the Creator of the Universe and His once-pure, pristine creation was instantly and finally... healed.

In the shadow of the blinding light of Yeshua's sacrifice lay the endless trail of dismembered carcasses from guiltless animals, slain for the flowing volumes of their innocent blood. Yet that crimson fluid—drained, poured, thrown and splashed about in the unceasing attempts to cover every kind of human offense, guilt and violation—had never been enough. Despite the mass of butchery, entrails and flesh leading to the base of that blood-stained stake, it had been impossible for the lives of goats or bulls to take away sins forever (Hebrews 10:4). No amount of life presented as compensation for mankind's mis-

---

[55] Some Hebrew manuscripts, one of the Dead Sea scrolls, and the Septuagint (the ancient Jewish translation of the Hebrew into Greek) say "piercing." Most Hebrew manuscripts say, "like a lion at." The difference between the two words is a single Hebrew letter "ו" (vav) or "י" (yud).

deeds could ever equal the perfect and pleasing self-sacrifice of the One in whom both humanity and God reside.

And beginning from the disobedience in the Garden…

…to the bringing of sin into the world…

…to the ungrateful grumbling of Israel…

…to the moral bankruptcy of her kings…

…to the refusal of God's chosen people to remain set apart for His purposes…

…to the sin of every individual man, woman, and child from every nation under heaven for all time…

…the *God of Atonement* could only accept—once and for all—the costly, bloody sacrificial death of this singular, incomparable Yeshua. Freely offering up Himself—trading His life for ours—the Messiah Yeshua paid a crushing debt that He never owed. And the *God of Love* redeemed that payment for the atonement and forgiveness of the entire world (cf. Leviticus 17:11, Hebrews 9:22).

> …the Messiah loved us and gave Himself for us—an offering and a sacrifice to God for a fragrance of a sweet smell. -Ephesians 5:2

> "For God so loved the world, that the Son—the one and only—He gave, so that everyone who is believing in Him may not be destroyed, but may have life everlasting. For God did not send the Son to the world so that He might judge the world, but so that the world might be saved through Him. He who is believing in Him is not judged, but he who is not believing has been judged already,

because he has not believed in the Name of the one and only Son of God." –John 3:16-18

And the earth quaked, and the rocks were cleaved, and the massive curtain of the Temple was split from top to bottom, as the Messiah Yeshua bowed His head and breathed out His last (Matthew 27:50f, Mark 15:37f, Luke 23:45f, John 19:30).

In fulfillment of the mediation and covenants of Israel, the door of reconciliation between God and man was thrown wide open forever. Everyone who now falls at the feet of Yeshua will be covered with the blameless blood of the Lamb of God. Their sins that are as scarlet will be eternally made white as snow (Isaiah 1:18).

It Is Finished

The people stood in astonishment and fear, having witnessed the terrifying spectacle. Still suspended above them was the lifeless body of their executed King, and before them, the aftermath of His violent and dramatic end. Some who had been watching were immediately filled with remorse and regret —their eyes opened to the atrocity that had just been perpetrated. Even as the people realized their grave mistake, saying, "Truly, this was God's Son" (Matthew 27:54), a soldier pierced Yeshua's side, and blood and water spilled out from His body upon the ground (John 19:34). The people returned home beating their chests in grief (Luke 23:48). The Son of God was dead.

> And they will have looked to Me whom they have
>   pierced,
> And they will have mourned over him
> As a mourning over an only son,
> And weeping bitterly over him

> As a bitter weeping over the firstborn.
>
> –Zechariah 12:10

Since it was the day before the Shabbat, one of the council members (who was a disciple of Yeshua, and had dissented over His death) received permission from the governor to take Yeshua's body for burial (Mark 15:42f, Luke 23:50ff). The councilor was a rich man, and donated his own tomb that had been newly cut out of a large mass of solid rock. That evening, Yeshua was wrapped in a clean linen shroud and laid inside the cavern, with a huge stone rolled in front of the entrance. The Jewish leadership—worried that the disciples would steal the body and then claim He had risen from the dead—secured the tomb, sealed the stone in place, and posted guards (Matthew 27:62ff).

After resting on the Shabbat as is commanded (Luke 23:56), several of the women headed to the garden tomb around dawn on the first day of the week (Mark 16:1f). Though they were expecting nothing more than to anoint the body for burial, there suddenly came a massive earthquake with a flash like lightning (Matthew 28:2f), and they saw that the tomb's heavy stone door had been rolled away. Disoriented and dismayed, they stumbled inside. To their horror, they did not find Yeshua's body and were afraid He had been taken (John 20:2). Yet as they looked on in wonderment—and as the guards shook with fear (Matthew 28:4)—they beheld a sight of angels from God who were declaring that the Crucified One was once again... *alive* (Luke 24:23). "Fear not!" came the exhortation. "Be not amazed." "Why do you look for the living among the dead? He is not here, but was raised!" (Matthew 28:5, Mark 16:6, Luke 24:5f).

By the extraordinary, explosive power of the Creator of all things, Yeshua forever defeated death and the authority of the grave. The Messiah abolished death's dominion—it being utterly unable to hold Him—and, for all who believe in His rising again, He put a permanent end to mortality's pain (1 Corinthians 15:42ff; Acts 2:24; 2 Timothy 1:10; Romans 6:9, 10:9f).

> "THE DEATH WAS SWALLOWED UP — TO VICTORY! WHERE, O DEATH, *IS* YOUR VICTORY? WHERE, O Death, *IS* YOUR STING?" -1 Corinthians 15:54-55[56]

> "And we proclaim Good News to you: that the promise made to the fathers — this, God has completed to us (their children) in full, having raised up Yeshua [from the dead]... -Acts 13:32-33

> For if, being enemies [of the Good News], we have been reconciled to God through the death of His Son, *then how* much more, having been reconciled, will we be saved in His life! -Romans 5:10

The God of Love gave His only Son in order to open the final, long-awaited, promised door to our reconciliation with Him. The sins that Yeshua took away from us and paid for though His death were exchanged for the eternal salvation that He offers us through His life. By His selfless, loving, one-of-a-kind sacrifice, Yeshua has led the way for us to emulate and follow: to be buried with Him in victory over sin, and to be raised up with Him in triumph over death (Romans 6:4-10).

For the next several weeks, the resurrected Yeshua frequently appeared to His disciples, doing many other signs (John 20:30) and offering many convincing proofs that He was real and human and scarred and alive (Luke 24:38ff, Acts 1:3). He also expounded to them all the things written about Himself in the

---

[56] Citing Isaiah 25:8 and Hosea 13:14

Scriptures, opening up their understanding beginning from the Torah, the Prophets, and the Psalms (Luke 24:27,44-45).

Finally, appearing to them one last time, the Messiah Yeshua commissioned His disciples to proclaim in His Name the release from sins and restoration to the Creator — beginning from Jerusalem, to Judea, and even to the end of the earth (Luke 24:47, Acts 1:8). And after bringing them outside the city, He turned to them and raised up His hands, and then the everlasting King of Israel—the Jewish Messiah, the eternal Son of God—blessed them, was lifted up, and ascended out of their sight to be seated upon His heavenly, never-ending throne (Luke 24:50f, Acts 1:9, Hebrews 8:1). The disciples bowed down in worship, and then returned to Jerusalem with overabounding happiness and joy. And from that day on they were continually in the Temple, proclaiming and blessing Israel's awesome, astounding, forgiving—and loving—God (Luke 24:52).

...these [things] have been written so that you may believe that Yeshua is the Messiah—the Son of God—and that, believing, you may have life in His Name. -John 20:31

CHAPTER 12

God of Reconciliation

The Good News returns us to God.

In the beginning, nothing stood between God and man. He made the man Adam and his wife, and then placed them in the middle of His perfect *creation*, providing for them everything they would ever need. Yet Adam would not do the one thing that God had asked of him: to trust His word and to choose life. Adam's disobedience brought sin, death and *judgment* to the world—unraveling man's close-knit relationship with God, barring access to the Tree of Life, and sentencing all humanity to separation from their Creator.

But there was Good News: the God of Reconciliation was already preparing another way back.

Adam's descendants multiplied, as did their inclination toward evil. Grieving at the abundant wickedness of man, God resolved to send a catastrophic flood to wipe out nearly every living creature on earth. He would, however, preserve the life of the world through the one righteous man, Noah. By way of God's lifeboat of *salvation*, humanity was given a second chance.

The children of Noah replenished the earth and divided into numerous nations. From that multitude, God set apart our father Abraham, through whose Hebrew progeny He *promised* to bless all the families of the world. In Abraham's son Isaac, and his son Jacob, God created His covenantal, chosen people. And in Jacob—who ultimately became Israel—God established His mediating nation for the restoration of everyone.

The house of Israel met with hardship and suffering. Diverted to Egypt, they soon found themselves captive to bitter slavery. But God remembered His promises and raised up Moses to *deliver* His people. Passing through doorways painted with lambs' innocent blood, the children of Israel were set free.

Upon arriving at the desert mountain, Israel was given God's *commands*—a Torah to guide them as His distinctive people. He taught them the difference between right and wrong, and how sin must be *atoned* for by the substitution of the sinless.

Yet the people quickly strayed from God's teaching. Rather than hear the word of the promise-keeper who had saved their lives, their desire was instead for the neighboring nations' wayward ways. Repeatedly, Israel turned from God and from their calling as His facilitators of world restoration. Yet for all their ungratefulness, rebelliousness, and breaking of faith, God remained *faithful* to broken Israel.

In their perpetual stubbornness, the people soon demanded a king in place of their God. But after giving them the ruler they so richly deserved, God then *redeemed* them with the one that they didn't. In David, the people found a champion, a protector, and God's unmerited favor, while God found a man after His own heart—a flawed trustee yet worthy of an eternal throne.

Through each of these, God was gradually *revealing* the means by which Israel would fulfill their sacred intercession for the world. With each stone that He laid, God was preparing the foundation for His chosen servant Israel to be that "kingdom of priests" and "holy nation" (Exodus 19:6). And yet, the people of God kept walking away. The nation divided. They were conquered and exiled from their land. The kingdom was left in ruin. Despite all that God had done to raise up His people, that permanent restoration between humanity and their Creator would be brought about by neither Noah nor Abraham, nor Isaac nor Jacob, nor Moses nor Torah, nor animal sacrifice nor David. Instead, standing firmly upon that Jewish foundation, the culmination of all God's promises, provision, patriarchs and kings was found in David's *son*—the son of Abraham, the son of Adam... the Son of God. Because God so *loved* the world, He finally brought forth the eternal prophet, priest and king of Israel—the cornerstone, the Master—the Messiah Yeshua.

The Good News

The Good News is a Jewish story about the Jewish people and their Jewish Messiah whom the God of Israel has sent to repair the world. While the message of the Good News speaks to the need of each individual soul of every nation, tribe and tongue, it is a message that nevertheless fundamentally relies upon God's foundational and continuing relationship with one particular, peculiar people: Israel. Yeshua's reconciling work on our behalf to make amends and to restore humanity's relationship with God is not true simply because it happened. It is true because God embedded and foreshadowed it in the story of His own Jewish people *according to their very own Scriptures*.

After the death, burial, resurrection and ascension of Yeshua, many tens of thousands of Jews—all of whom were zealous for the Torah—believed (Acts 21:20). One of the instrumental voices in spreading the word was the persuasive and prolific

Paul, a member of the Jewish religious order of the Pharisees and a former persecutor of Jewish followers of Yeshua. After a dramatic encounter with the risen Messiah, Paul instantly became a fervent and devout emissary for the message of the Good News. Writing to the believers in the Grecian city of Corinth, Paul encapsulates the Good News this way:

> And I make known to you, brothers, the Good News that I proclaimed to you, which you also received, in which you also have stood, *and* through which you are also being saved.... For I delivered to you first what I also received: that Messiah died for our sins according to the Scriptures, and that He was buried, and that He has risen on the third day according to the Scriptures....
> –1 Corinthians 15:1-4

This is the essential Gospel according to Israel. Though not immediately obvious in his statement, Paul implicitly ties the Good News of Yeshua to the Jewish people.

That "Messiah died for our sins" and that "He was buried" and "has risen" from the dead is the core and all-encompassing truth of the Good News. This is the sacrifice and mediation that has made the reconciliation between God and man possible—an eternally opened door through which all may enter, return to Paradise, and no longer be separated from their Creator. But it was not just any Messiah who died and rose again. It was namely the son of David. And it was not just any death and resurrection that happened to be announced beforehand through the prophets of God (Romans 1:1f). It was the one and only Messiah Yeshua who died, was buried, and rose from the dead for our sins because that was God's remedy for us "according to the Scriptures"—*according to the Scriptures of Israel.*

Without the Hebrew Scriptures—without the covenants, the sacrifices, and the people-group to whom God has forever attached His Name (Ezekiel 36:22f)—the Good News is a house of cards. Paul, in fact, establishes this in the opening of his letter to the believers in Rome, stating that the Jews hold the foundational position in relation to the salvation of the world. "The Good News," he says, "is the power of God to salvation to everyone who is believing... to the Jew first" (Romans 1:16). He even goes on to assert that it is the people of Israel to whom belong God's "adoption *as sons*, and the glory, and the covenants, and the Torah-giving, and the service, and the promises; *also* whose ARE the fathers; and of whom... IS the Messiah" Himself (9:4f). If the Good News of Yeshua—which *is* the power of God to salvation—is not first for the Jew, then it is never for anyone. If the Messiah Yeshua is not the embodiment of His Jewish people and their national servant-role to the world, and if He did not specifically enact and bring the Hebrew Scriptures to their fullness, then He suffered, died, rose for—and reconciled—nobody.

Covenant Doors

The reliance of the Good News on God's history with Israel is evident from the beginning. From the moment of Adam's banishment out of the garden and the shutting of the gate behind him, the God of Reconciliation began opening a series of steadily narrowing doorways back to Himself—a pathway leading straight to the feet of Yeshua, paved with the covenants of Israel.

With Noah, God opened the saving *door of the ark* before the destruction of the world, and then covenanted to never again send a flood to devastate the earth.

With Abraham, Isaac and Jacob, God opened the *door of Israel's founding patriarchs*, establishing an everlasting covenant of promise for a Land and a people, through whom all the nations of the earth would be blessed.

With Moses, God opened the *doors of the Passover*—bloodstained passageways that shielded Israel by night, and through which the people were freed at the coming of the day. God also opened the *door of substitutionary sacrifice* and an intercessory priesthood, given at the heart of the covenant of Torah — instructions by which to fulfill their collective, priestly calling.

With David, God opened the *door of an eternal throne*, establishing a covenant with the messianic king for a house and a kingdom forever.

And with Yeshua, God rolled opened the *door of the garden tomb*, defeating sin and death on our behalf, and, in His blood, ratifying the New Covenant that God had finally made with the house of Israel and the house of Judah.

Without each and every covenantal door that God ultimately placed before Israel, humanity would have remained forever without access or a way back to our Creator. Before Yeshua could accomplish His singular sacrificial act of reconciliation, each door first needed to be opened.

Without the door of the ark, humanity would have been cut off from salvation—swept away into oblivion, never to return to God. Without the patriarchs' door, there would be no promises from God, and no way to fulfill them in Abraham's seed. Without the Passover door, Israel would have been left imprisoned and in slavery, with no precedent for the shedding of blood that sets people free. Without the door of substitutionary sacrifice there would be no acceptance of the life of innocents in exchange for the deathly consequences of sin. Without the door of David's eternal throne, there would be no everlasting Kingdom at hand, and no eternal King who could bring us near —even now—to the endless reality and glory of God.

And without the door of the garden tomb, there would be no Messiah to fulfill the covenants that God made with His chosen Jewish people, no Master to lead and enable Israel in the accomplishment of their national mission to the nations, and no Savior to remedy what Adam wrought for humanity, completing God's compassionate and merciful work for the once-and-for-all salvation and reconciliation of the world.

The Righteousness of God

As sons of Adam, we are each heirs of his shortcomings, his weakness, and his fate. Since "by the misstep of the one *man* the death reigned" through him, therefore "the death also passed through to all men, in that all sinned" (Romans 5:17&12). God, then, "does not hear sinners" (John 9:31) and can have no relationship with us, because he "who is doing the sin is of the Accuser"—that diabolical serpent who has been sinning "from the beginning" (1 John 3:8). Our expelled, mortal flesh has consequently inherited its great susceptibility to temptation and its irresistible propensity toward sin. For this reason, "the mind of the flesh *is* death"—it is "hostility to God" (Romans 8:6-7), naturally unable to obey Him and abound in His presence.

Since this is the unavoidable, irreversible, irreparable condition of humanity, and because God is gracious and overabundant in forgiveness and love, this is why He sent to us the Messiah Yeshua—to finally make things right. Paul writes,

> For in our still being weak, Messiah—in due time—died for the ungodly. For with difficulty will anyone die for a righteous man; indeed, for the good man, perhaps someone even dares to die. But God proves His own love to us: that, in our still being sinners, Messiah died for us. *How* much more, then, having now been declared righteous in His blood, will we be saved through Him from the wrath! For if, being enemies, we have been reconciled to God through the death of His Son, *then how* much more, having been reconciled, will we be saved in His life! –Romans 5:6-10

In our incurable condition as willful sinners, we are enemies of God. We do not listen to or obey His word. We stand against Him. We violate His standards of righteousness, making us deserving of wrath, punishment and death. But while we are in that state of weakness—without any ability within ourselves to overcome it—the God of Reconciliation has worked out a way to accept a restitution on our behalf that satisfies His requirements for justice. Namely, "in our still being sinners, Messiah died for us." Through Yeshua's death, by His sinless blood—by His taking our place in death, which we owe for our own wrongdoing—we are now considered and declared, "Righteous!" By Yeshua's dying for us, we are reconciled to our Creator; by His resurrected life, we are made right with God, and are saved.

This was the sacrifice that God had always needed and intended to offer. Like our father Abraham, the Father of us all proved His love for us by giving the life of His Son. And like Abraham's son Isaac—willing to lay upon the altar, trusting in his father's word—this was the atonement that was always Yeshua's honor and joy to make.

> [In Yeshua] it pleased all the fullness *of the Deity* to dwell and, through Him, to reconcile all the things to Himself, having made peace through the blood of His *execution* stake; *all are reconciled* through Him, whether the things on the earth or the things in the heavens. And you, once being alienated and enemies in the mind, *engaged* in the evil actions; yet now He reconciled *you* in the body of His flesh through the death, *in order* to present you *as* holy and unblemished and unblameable before Himself... –Colossians 1:19-22

Despite the excruciating, torturous, and agonizing execution He endured, it nevertheless pleased Yeshua to be the instrument of our reconciliation. Through the Messiah's broken body and the spilling of His innocent blood, Yeshua restored the ancient, long-lost peace between humanity and God... no longer alienated and detached from Him, no longer banned from His presence, no longer His enemies.

Such an extreme measure was necessary to take on our account because no effort of ourselves can ever make us sufficiently moral or clean or pure, either to exempt us from the deathly cost of our sin, or to make us acceptable to stand before a holy God. Instead, Yeshua reconciled *our* sin in *His* body in order to lawfully present us not as those who are defiled by sin—not as ones who have accrued the stains of guilt—but as those whose debt is wiped away, *fully paid*. Therefore, for those in Yeshua, having been made holy, unblemished, and considered to be completely without blame, the irreparable condition of our sinful humanity is not *repaired*, but *replaced*. In Messiah, we are *remade* completely new. Paul declares,

> Therefore, if anyone *IS* in Messiah, *HE IS* a new creature; the old things *have* passed away; look! he has become

> new! And all the things ARE of God, who reconciled us to Himself through Messiah and gave to us the service of the reconciliation, such that God was reconciling the world to Himself in Messiah, not counting their missteps against them, and has put in us the word of the reconciliation.... We implore *you* for the sake of Messiah: "Be reconciled to God." *God* made Him who did not know sin *to be* sin for our sake, so that we may become the righteousness of God in Him. –2 Corinthians 5:17-21

Unlike the sin offering and the blood of bulls and goats, which does not last, the endless blood of the Messiah Yeshua accomplishes a once-and-for-all atonement, leaving us permanently covered and clean. While Israel's High Priest would enter into the Tent of Meeting's holy places repeatedly—"every year with *the* blood of others"—Yeshua entered not into "holy places made with hands... but into Heaven itself," and He entered there but *a single time*, with *His very own blood*, for the complete and final "nullification of sin through His sacrifice" (Hebrews 9:11-26). Because of that nullification, we who are in Messiah are no longer bound and enslaved to sin. Instead, like Israel leaving Egypt, our old things have passed away forever. In the service of the Messiah's reconciliation, the person we used to be—sinful, selfish, separated from God—is no more. And with that old self dead, buried, and left behind, we become new! We are made a brand new creature in Messiah, raised with Him from the dead, and recreated in His image, so that we may return to God and walk with Him in the newness of life. No longer does He count our past missteps against us, but forgives what we owe, forgets it for good, and receives us to Himself in full reconciliation.

What God did through Yeshua closed the chasm between us and our Creator which was formed and sustained because of humanity's sin. He did this by making the One who had never known sin "*to be* sin for our sake"—to become the thing of despisement and hostility that cuts us off from God. Yeshua took our place, He paid our price, He sacrificed His life for ours, and He released us from our obligation to death, eternal punishment, and separation from God. And He did this not only so that we could be brought near—not only so that we might receive the promise of an eternal inheritance (9:15)—but so that we could be made new, turn away from sin, and become "the righteousness of God in Him."

Life from the Dead

It is in that righteousness, then — that uprightness, that right relationship with God, that awakened inclination to habitually choose to do what is right in God's eyes — that we find the importance and purpose for our new life.

And this is especially true for the Jew.

Yeshua not only gives the Jewish believer—like all believers—direction for his life, a reason for living, a goal for eternity, and a desire for personal holiness. He also restores the Jew to his ancient function as a member of God's uniquely "chosen ancestry" and "kingdom of priests"—a "people treasured *as God's own*" (1 Peter 2:9). As the national facilitators of salvation for the world—as "a holy priesthood [built] to offer up spiritual sacrifices" to God on behalf of the nations (2:5)—the Jew receives back his long-lost purpose as a child of Israel.

Paul not only understood this purpose, but embodied it. In every city of the Roman world where He traveled to proclaim the Good News, he would always go first to the Jews. But while some did believe, many more rejected the message of eternal life and of their own Jewish Messiah. Consequently,

Paul turned to the Gentiles. In agreement with Yeshua's own declaration that "salvation is of the Jews" (John 4:22), Paul saw this Jewish mission and calling to the nations expressly stated by the prophet Isaiah.

> "For so has ADONAI commanded us [Jews]: 'I have set you as a light for *the* Gentiles—for your being for salvation to the end of the earth.'" –Acts 13:47, cf. Isaiah 49:6

While Paul's heart remained perpetually and deeply burdened for the salvation of his own people (Romans 10:1), he nevertheless knew that, as a Jew, his ultimate purpose was to take that righteousness he had become, and to shine it to the end of the earth. Israel's righteousness and glory was always meant to be telegraphed to and seen by the nations (Isaiah 62:2). They would hear of God's statutes and judgments given to Israel. They would be amazed at Israel's wisdom, understanding and nearness to their God (Deuteronomy 4:6f). Paul knew that this age-old mandate needed to be fulfilled by him and every other Jew—not as an upstanding citizen of foreign lands, or as an innovator in the arts or sciences, or as a philanthropist or celebrated luminary, but only as a representative of the Messiah Yeshua and of the holy nation and priestly kingdom of Israel. Paul's ambition was to be a beacon of righteousness to light the way to Yeshua, and thereby mediate the world's salvation.

And yet, Paul still saw his own individual role in this as limited. He knew that while the rejection of Yeshua among his people led him to turn to the Gentiles (whom he found massively receptive to the Good News), the abundant fruit produced among them still fell far short of what it will one day be once all Israel is saved (Romans 11:26). Though Paul's efforts would help bring about and instigate a widespread *reconciliation*, Israel's salvation will finally result in worldwide *resurrection*.

> And if [Israel's] misstep *is* the riches of the world, and their diminishing *is* the riches of *the* Gentiles, how much more *will* [Israel's] fullness *be*?... For if their rejection [of Messiah] *is* a reconciliation of the world, what *will* their reception [of Him] *be* if not life out of the dead?
> –Romans 11:12&15

The Jewish people's partial and temporary hardening toward Yeshua afforded Paul the personal opportunity to take the Good News to the Gentile world. This was the "riches" and the reconciliation that he was witnessing among them — an inheritance and birthright which many Jews (like Esau before them) were still forsaking. Yet that sweeping "reconciliation of the world," which was and is being accomplished while Jews largely reject their Messiah, will pale in comparison to what is set to take place at Israel's eventual "fullness" and "reception" of Him. The Jewish people's collective salvation will mean the greatest, most explosive and effective spreading of the Good News in the history of humanity. It will be the consummate, conclusive resurrection of the world — a *super-reconciliation* among those being saved. "Life out of the dead" is what the Jew was born for.

This is the reason why each of us are made "a new creature" and "the righteousness of God" in Messiah (2 Corinthians 5:17,21). Our individual purpose is to shine and share the light of Yeshua's salvation. We are each to proclaim and live out the truth and reality of the Good News and the word of God within our spheres of influence—through our speech, our changed behavior, and the inward transformation that comes "by the renewing of the mind" (Romans 12:2). But only when that very "righteousness of God" is finally reflected in a single, unified Jewish people—able to keep the covenant of blessing to all the families of the earth (Genesis 12:3), able to fulfill their ancient vow, "All that ADONAI has spoken we will do" (Exodus 19:8)—then the sign of Israel receiving the Messiah *en masse* will draw the world to God like never before. Without the salvation of the Jewish people, the reconciliation of the world will forever remain unfinished. Since the beginning, this has always been God's plan: He will use His chosen servant Israel, in Messiah, to change the world.

> In those coming *days*, Jacob will take root,
> Israel will blossom and will have sent out shoots,
> And they will have filled the face of the world WITH
> *fruitful* increase.
> –Isaiah 27:6

The Gospel according to Israel is a Jewish story about the Jewish Messiah which relies on the Jewish people and the covenants that God made and keeps with them. But for the Jewish person, it is even more than that. It also gives us our life's purpose. It tells us who we truly are, what God has uniquely made us to do, and everything that is necessary to do it. In Yeshua, we Jews find the personified completion of our God-given, collective mission. And in Him, we receive the needed cleansing of our sins, the righteousness of God, and the new and eternal life to fulfill it. Though the God of Reconciliation needs neither man nor nation to reconcile people to Himself, He nevertheless chose us, Israel — His peculiar, Jewish nation — to bear the responsibility. We are the means and vehicle by which He will save the world: a reconciliation accomplished in the embodiment of the Messiah Yeshua; a reconciliation broadcast to all the earth through the righteous light of His life-bringing, messianic people.

CHAPTER 13

God of Life

The Good News makes all things new.

Paul would continue to travel and faithfully proclaim the Good News even at great cost to himself. During the first of his many imprisonments, a midnight earthquake rocked the foundation of the jail, every door was instantly flung open, and each prisoner's bonds were miraculously loosed. The jailer, having witnessed the wondrous sign, turned to Paul and cried out to him, "What must I do—that I may be saved?" To this, Paul replied by showing him the true path of salvation and the simple way of the Good News, "Believe in the Master Yeshua, and you will be saved" (Acts 16:26-31).

Like the jailer, and Paul, and everyone who has ever lived and ever will live, so it is for you. Your sinful actions (done intentionally or in ignorance), your violations against God's word, and your accrued guilt—these all make you deserving of permanent separation from God... worthy of death and eternal fiery punishment (Matthew 25:41-46). No amount of good deeds you can do, or points you can earn, will be able to dig you out of that hole and repay your unaffordable debt. But because of Yeshua's self-sacrifice on your behalf, if you believe, the God of Life is able to give you what you do *not* deserve—what your life does *not* merit. "For by *unmerited* favor you are having been saved, through faith, and this not of *something* you *did—it is* the gift of God, not of *your* actions—so that no one may boast" (Ephesians 2:8-9). Salvation is an unearned gift from God. It is available to you not because of your actions, but in spite of them.

Your salvation is based solely on whether you believe the Good News that the Messiah Yeshua died for your sins, was buried, and rose from the dead on the third day according to the Scriptures (1 Corinthians 15:1ff). Yeshua taught us that the way to enter eternal life and to find salvation is not through reciting the right prayers, or performing the correct rituals, or doing acts of charity or contrition, or being a "good" person, but simply *through Him*. He said, "I am the door. If anyone comes in through Me, he will be saved" (John 10:9). The door is now unlocked and open. There is nothing standing between you and your reconciliation. Redemption through Yeshua is just a threshold away.

Even Moses taught us that such accessibility to God is within our reach. In his instructions about the voice and Torah of ADONAI, Moses exhorted the people of Israel to hear and do God's word. He taught them that even though it can seem arduous and overwhelming, in reality, "it is not too difficult for you." It is not far away or hard to get, such that you need someone else to go up to heaven or across the sea to retrieve and bring it back for you. Instead, "the word is exceedingly near to you, in your mouth and in your heart." God has already placed it within you (Deuteronomy 30:11-14). You are able to draw "near, then—unhindered—to the throne of *unmerited* favor, so that [you] may receive *loving*-kindness and find *unmerited* favor—for timely help" (Hebrews 4:16). This access and nearness that Moses says we have to God's word is the very same access and nearness that you can have with the one and only Word of God. The mouth and heart which proclaims that *you are fully able to do God's word* is the very same mouth and heart which speaks with the confidence of faith that *you can believe and be saved*. Paul puts it like this:

> ...that if you confess with your mouth, "Yeshua *is* Master," and believe in your heart that God raised Him out of the dead, you will be saved. For with the heart ONE believes, *leading* to righteousness; and with the mouth confession is made, *leading* to salvation. For the Scripture says, "EVERYONE WHO IS BELIEVING ON HIM WILL NOT BE ASHAMED." –Romans 10:9-11, cf. Isaiah 28:16

Entrance through the door of Yeshua, and the erasure of your shame, is granted because of faith—because you believe the Good News. It is not your actions that make you righteous and clean; rather, it is the knowing and acceptance in your heart that Yeshua died for your sins and was raised from the dead. It is not the balance of your virtue that saves you, with your good deeds outweighing the bad; rather, it is your mouth's confession of the heart and profession of the truth that Yeshua is now your Master. It is a salvation that is free—it cannot be earned, bought or sold; it requires nothing of you but your belief.

What You Lose, What You Gain

And yet, though the gift itself is free, the new life that comes with it is *not free* from boundaries, sacrifice and commitment. When you receive God's glorious and unearned reconciliation, it does come at a cost.

When you agree to accept Yeshua's gift—His taking your place and suffering the consequences that you deserve—you will no longer be your own. You will have been bought with a price—

redeemed with the precious blood of the Messiah (1 Corinthians 6:19f, 1 Peter 1:19). Your ownership will change hands. You will be freed from being a slave of sin, bound to its influence and abuse, and instead become a slave to righteousness and God (Romans 6:17-22), whose "commands are not burdensome" (1 John 5:3), and whose yoke is easy and load is light (Matthew 11:30).

Your life, then—at one time forfeit forever to sin and death—will belong to Yeshua. In humble submission to your Master, the new life you will then be able to live in Him will gain you, and cost you... everything. As Yeshua teaches us,

> "If anyone wants to follow after Me, let him deny himself, and take up his *execution* stake, and follow Me; for whoever wants to save his life will lose it; and whoever loses his life for My sake and the Good News' sake, will save it." –Mark 8:34-35

The unselfish response to the One who unselfishly gave Himself for you is to give yourself up entirely for Him. On the Day of Atonement (Leviticus 23:26ff), we catch a glimpse of this self-denial as we temporarily afflict our souls by refusing ourselves sustenance. But the eternal atonement made by Messiah's sinless sacrifice—His becoming the ransom for us all, destroying the power of death and the Accuser, and delivering you from bondage and slavery (Hebrews 2:6&14f)—is it not easily worth infinitely more than the self-denial of the rest of your life? To fully enter into the salvation of Yeshua, you will need to forsake your sinful pleasures, realign your preferences and priorities with God's word, leave your old self and self-interests behind, accept your new identity in Yeshua, follow Him wholeheartedly, and give your life freely to His cause and your calling. To deny yourself and to be saved through Messiah is to accept that you have been "born *again* from above" (John 3:3ff)—that you have been crucified with Him and the old *you* no longer lives. The life you can now live will be because Messiah lives in you—because He loved you and gave Himself for you (Galatians 2:19f).

Is the cost of your self too much to ask from the One who takes away your sin, redeems your soul from death, and reconciles you to your Maker for eternity?

Should you choose, then, to follow the selfless, self-sacrificial Yeshua, you will be expected to follow His example: to deny yourself and to devote to Him everything you are (Luke 14:33). But what you give up by losing your life to serve the Master is *nothing* compared to the immeasurable benefits that you will gain in Him. When you give yourself to Yeshua, first—but not least—He saves you, and takes away your sin.

> And so all Israel will be saved, as it has been written, "There will come forth out of Zion he who is delivering; he will turn away ungodliness from Jacob. And this is the covenant from Me to them, when I take away their sins."
> –Romans 11:26-27, cf. Isaiah 27:9, 59:20-21; Jeremiah 31:33-34

When you give yourself to Yeshua and own up to your unrighteousness, His blood will cleanse you, and you will be forgiven for every sin you ever made (1 John 1:7f). As our merciful and faithful High Priest, Yeshua can also sympathize with your weaknesses, having been "tempted in all things likewise *as we are*," yet having remained "apart from sin" (Hebrews 4:14f). As the mediator of a new and better covenant, Yeshua is able to make appeasement for all your wrongdoing (Hebrews 2:17, 8:6, 9:15). He will blot out those accusations against you, take them out of the way, nail them to the execution stake, and then forgive and forget (Colossians 2:13f, Hebrews 10:16ff). Yeshua will wash you clean from all your uncleannesses, and take away your heart of stone. In its place He will give you a fresh, pure, new heart of flesh, and put a brand new spirit within you (Ezekiel 36:25f). When you confess and believe in Yeshua, you will no longer owe any wages to the work of sin and death. Your body will die and your soul will face judgment, yet you will not be sent away to be destroyed forever in fire. Instead, you will be raised and reconciled to a right relationship with your Creator, having been given the free gift of God: eternal and everlasting life (John 3:16, Romans 6:23).

> And I saw a new heaven and a new earth—for the first heaven and the first earth went away, and the sea is not anymore. And I saw the holy city—the New Jerusalem—coming down out of the heaven from God, made ready as a bride arranged for her husband. And I heard a loud voice from the throne, saying, "Look! the tent of God *is* with men, and He will dwell with them, and they will be His peoples, and God Himself will be with them *and be* their God, and He will wipe away every tear from their eyes, and death will not be anymore, nor mourning, nor crying, nor will there be any more pain, because the first things went away." And He who is sitting upon the throne said, "Look! I make all things new." –Revelation 21:1-5, cf. Leviticus 26:11; Isaiah 25:8, 65:17-19

For those who are in Messiah, at the end of our days we will find ourselves away from the body and at home with our God, our true citizenship being with Him in the Heavens forever (Philippians 3:20, cf. 2 Corinthians 5:6ff). The splendor and magnificence of that spectacle will be beyond description; the peace, restoration and joy beyond compare. In the New Jerusalem, there will be no Temple, for its Temple will be God Himself and the Lamb. There will be no need for either Sun or Moon, for

God's glory will illuminate every corner of creation. The gates of the city will never be shut because there will be no night, and nothing impure or false will enter in. "*Only* those written in the Book of the Life of the Lamb" will go through, and will fully and finally know the one true God of Life (Revelation 21:22-27, Jeremiah 31:34, John 17:3).

The scales of loss and gain in Messiah are immeasurably weighted in your favor. Nothing that this earth can offer you during your brief existence here can even begin to compare to the abundance in Yeshua—both in this life now and in the life to come. Yes, you will incur a cost—the loss of your freedom to sin, to serve yourself, and to live as you please. But in Yeshua, you will find the freedom and wholeness that can only be purchased on your behalf by the Messiah's excruciating pain, agonizing suffering, and selfless sacrifice. The Master Yeshua has made a way—the only way—to reconciliation and life everlasting. He says, "I am the way, and the truth, and the life; no one comes to the Father unless through Me" (John 14:6). Yeshua has opened the door. You only need to walk through.

Will you now take that step of faith, and enter in?

What You Should Do

At the time of Yeshua's breathtaking ascension, it was just days away from the next pilgrimage Feast: Shavuot. Jews from every nation under heaven—including Yeshua's disciples and emissaries—were arriving and going up to Jerusalem, entering the courts of the House of God. On the day of the harvest feast, as all Israel was gathered, the sound of a driving, violent breath suddenly filled the Temple. Instantly, each of the disciples began speaking aloud the great things of God—praising Him miraculously in languages that they themselves did not speak, but that their visiting fellow Jews heard in their own dialects. Confounded, confused and amazed, the people did not know what to make of the heavenly sign they were witnessing. So the disciples rose up—emboldened by the Holy Spirit—and began proclaiming the message of sacrifice, salvation and reconciliation through the crucified Messiah Yeshua (Acts 2:1-36).

> And having heard, [the people] were pierced to the heart, *and* they also said to Peter and to the remainder of the emissaries, "What should we do, men? brothers?" And Peter said to them, "Repent, and be immersed, each of you, in the Name of Yeshua *the* Messiah, to *the* release of your sins; and you will receive the gift of the Holy Spirit." Then those, indeed, who received his word were immersed [in water], and there were added on that day about three thousand [Jewish] souls. –Acts 2:37-38&41

The thousands of devout Jews that day were "pierced to the heart" not only because they realized that God had repudiated their rejection of His Son — having confirmed Yeshua as their Messiah and King by raising Him from the dead — but also because they were grieved that they had turned away the Son of David and the means of their own salvation.

When you truly believe in the Master Yeshua—when you comprehend the dire gravity of your sin, the utter foolishness and depravity of your actions, the sheer weight of the guilt that Yeshua took upon Himself, and the torturous punishment and death that He endured to free you from it—you will likewise be pierced to the heart. But the God of Life does not rejoice in your shame, regret and grief. He rejoices when your grief brings you to the point of *repentance* (2 Corinthians 7:9).

By feeling that deep sorrow and remorse over your past sinful actions, a change is meant to be enacted in your thinking — a reformation of your heart and mind — that drives you to turn aside from your old ways and the path of death, and to turn toward salvation and the way of life. You have lied, you have stolen, you have lusted, you have been sexually promiscuous. You have hated, you have mistreated others, you have raged in anger and acted without self-control. You have been impure, arrogant, and drunken; you have sown in evil and reaped in self-debasement. You have ignored or despised your Messiah, and have brushed off creation's plain evidence of the power and perfection of your God. But as a potter can remake a marred and corrupted vessel that he holds tenderly in his hands (Jeremiah 18:4-6), so can God take you in your brokenness and reform you, changing you into someone whole and good and useful. The grief toward God that leads to salvation is your genuine and sincere repentance.

What, then, must you now do?

To be saved, you must believe. "If you confess with your mouth, 'Yeshua *is* Master,' and believe in your heart that God raised Him out of the dead, you will be saved" (Romans 10:9). Accept the sacrifice that the Messiah Yeshua made on your behalf, and then humbly walk through the Door that He has opened for you.

To be forgiven, you must repent. "Repent, therefore, and return, for *the* blotting out *of* your sins, *so* that times of refreshing may come from the presence of ADONAI" (Acts 3:19f). Own up to your wrongdoing, be truly remorseful for your unrighteous ways, and confess your sins to God. Then ask Him to forgive you through the blood of the Lamb, and God will be "faithful [to] forgive [all your] sins and cleanse [you] from every unrighteousness" (1 John 1:9).

And to be reconciled — to fulfill the purpose God has had for you from before you were born — you must die to your old ways and turn from your sin. "Therefore, O house of Israel, I will judge you each according to his ways.... Return and turn yourselves back from all your violations, and *then* guilt will not be a stumbling-block to you. Throw off from yourselves all your violations by which you have sidestepped, and make to yourselves a new heart and a new spirit" (Ezekiel 18:30-31). When you are in Yeshua, you are reborn a new creation: the old has gone; the new has come (2 Corinthians 5:17). Having, therefore, been set free forever from sin and death, you must choose to live like it. Rather than remain shackled to your former corrupt behavior, repeating and remaining in your sin, you must throw off the "old self," and be "renewed in the spirit of your mind," putting on the "new self" of godliness and righteousness (Ephesians 4:22-24). Follow the example of Yeshua, walk in the Spirit, and adhere to the commands and teachings of God's word—the Bible. Clean out the old leaven of evil and wickedness, and "keep the Feast" with the matzah of purity and truth (1 Corinthians 5:7f).

By reaching out to God in your uncleanness, guilt, and shame, you take the step of faith that God is truly near — that He is ready and willing to make you clean, to save you, to forgive you, to heal the rift between you and Him, and to restore you to the purpose for which you were made. If you are hungry, come now to the Tree of Life, and eat; if you are thirsty, come to the river of living water and drink! Even before you call out to God, He will answer; while you are still speaking, He will hear (Isaiah 65:24). You are not alone. Indeed, when David the King finally felt the full weight of his own selfish, adulterous, murderous sin, He also cried out to God from the very depths of his soul. This is the way David prayed, and it can be your prayer, too:

> Show me mercy, O God, according to Your *loving-kindness*;
> According to the abundance of your compassion,
> Blot out my violations.
>
> Thoroughly wash me from my guilt,
> And cleanse me from my sin,
> For I know my violations,
> And my sin *is* continually before me.
>
> Against You... I have sinned
> And done evil in Your eyes,
> So that You are righteous in Your speaking;
> You are pure in Your judging.
>
> Look! I have been brought forth in guilt,
> And in sin my mother had conceived me.
> Look! You have delighted in truth in the inward parts,
> And in the hidden part You cause me to know wisdom.
>
> You cleanse me with hyssop and I am clean;
> You wash me, and I become whiter than snow.
> You cause me to hear joy and gladness;
> *The* bones You have crushed rejoice.
>
> Hide Your face from my sin,
> And blot out all my *causes of* guilt.
> Create for me a clean heart, O God,
> And renew a right spirit within me.

> Do not cast me away from Your presence,
> And do not take Your Holy Spirit from me.
> Restore to me the joy of Your salvation,
> And *let* a willing spirit sustain me.
>
> I will teach sidesteppers Your ways,
> And sinners will return to You.
> Deliver me from bloodguilt, O God, God of my salvation;
> My tongue will shout aloud of Your righteousness.
>
> O Adonai, open my lips,
> And my mouth will declare Your praise.
>
> –Psalm 51:1-15[3-17]

The emissary to the dispersed ones of Israel exhorts us,

> Blessed *is* the God and Father of our Master Yeshua *the* Messiah—who... brought us forth again to a living hope through the Rising Again of Yeshua *the* Messiah out of the dead, to an inheritance immortal and undefiled and unfading, reserved in the Heavens for you.... In this you are *being* extremely joyful... receiving the goal of your faith: salvation of *your* souls.
>
> Concerning this salvation.... [it] was revealed to [the prophets] that they were serving these *things* not to themselves, but to you—*things* which are now told to you through those who proclaimed Good News....
>
> Therefore... hope perfectly on the *unmerited* favor that is being brought to you in the revelation of Yeshua *the* Messiah as obedient children — not conforming yourselves to the former lusts in your ignorance. But as He

who called you *is* holy, you also, become holy in all behavior, because it has been written [in the Torah],

"Become holy, because I am holy."[57]

And if you call on the Father (who is judging without partiality, according to the action of each *person*), pass the time of your sojourn [in this world] having known that not with perishable things—silver or gold—were you redeemed from your foolish behavior handed down *to you* by *your* fathers, but with precious blood, as of a lamb unblemished and unspotted—Messiah's!

...Having purified your souls... be[] born again (not out of mortal seed, but immortal) through a word of God— living and remaining.... And this is the spoken word that was proclaimed *as* Good News to you." -1 Peter 1:3-25

The Master Yeshua is waiting for you. The covenantal doors are open; you have been shown the Way back to God... you have heard the Gospel according to Israel.

The God of Life has brought you to this moment; now it is time for you to make your decision. You have an ancient purpose with an eternal goal. The King of the Universe is calling you. How will you choose to answer?

Be reconciled to God. Come now to Yeshua... and choose *life*.

See, I have set before you today life and good, and death and evil.... the blessing and the curse. So choose life, so that you will live.... -Deuteronomy 30:15&19

---

[57] Leviticus 11:44,45; 19:2; 20:7

Epilogue

In the decade following Yeshua's resurrection and ascension, the Master was continually adding to the already many-thousand-fold Jewish followers of "The Way" (Acts 2:47, 9:2). While public favor toward this growing Jewish sect would begin to fade as their persecution by Israel's religious groups began to escalate (6:9ff, 8:1ff, 9:1f), the Good News of the Jewish Messiah was already spreading quickly to the Gentiles.

At first, receptive non-Jews were found among the "God-fearers"—those Gentiles who sought to worship the God of Israel, and who maintained a good reputation and relationship among the Jewish people (10:2&22). Later in his travels, Paul taught both Jews and Gentiles together, often warning against the legalistic misuse of the Torah, while simultaneously championing the perpetual holiness, righteousness and goodness of its commands (Romans 7:12). For another ten to fifteen years, the message of Israel's Messiah was retained and shared in its authentic Jewish framework. Paul would contextualize it for an uninitiated Gentile audience who previously knew nothing of Israel's God, and did "not have the Torah" (2:14).

Soon, however, tensions began to rise between the Jewish and Gentile believers. As reported especially in Paul's letter to the believing community in Rome, the two groups began to develop an arrogance and animosity toward one another and to divide into factions. The Jewish believers had grown prideful of their heritage, finding reason to boast in the distinctiveness of their Torah-keeping and circumcision (2:11ff). The Gentile believers returned the conceit in kind, considering themselves to be more favored by God because of their vastly growing numbers, which quickly dwarfed that of the Jewish believers. This anti-Jewish haughtiness was an ominous development that extended also to the whole of the people of Israel (11:1-36). It foreshadowed what would become the prevailing prejudice and supersessionist attitude of historical Christianity toward Jews for the next two thousand years.

In less than a generation, Jerusalem and the Temple were once again destroyed, and the Jewish people—including Jewish believers—were scattered. The relatively young movement of Messianic Jews found themselves no longer welcome among their own people, and fast losing influence among the believers...

...believers now increasingly dominated by distinctly non-Jewish Christians.

A Light to the Gentiles

There is no denying that since the end of the first century, it has been nearly unheard of for Jews to believe that Yeshua is the Messiah. The development of the new and separate religion of Christianity—often hateful and hostile to Jews, inexcusably so—shrouded and severed the Jewish Yeshua from His Jewish people.

Yet the overwhelming number of Christian followers of Israel's Messiah neither undermines nor negates Yeshua's legitimacy as Messiah, nor is it reason for Jews to *disbelieve* in Him. On the contrary, it is cause for *belief!* Why? Because God's aim for humanity's reconciliation has always been for *all* peoples. Indeed, Yeshua's salvation of the Gentiles is in direct fulfillment of the prophet's words to Israel.

> "For My House will be called 'a house of prayer' for **all the peoples**" — an utterance of the Lord God, who is gathering the outcasts of Israel—"yet others I will gather to him *and* to his gathered ones." -Isaiah 56:7-8

Adonai declares that His House—the Temple, which is exclusive to Israel—would one day permit people from *all* nations to enter and come near to Him. No longer relegated to an outer court, these "others" will be gathered to those of Israel whom He has already gathered. But why would the God of Israel suddenly welcome foreigners into His presence? Why would unsanctified outsiders now be accepted as holy? For the very same reason the Master Yeshua proclaims that there are "others" besides the Jewish people whom He also came to shepherd.

> "I am the good shepherd, and I know My sheep and My sheep know Me, as the Father knows Me and I know the Father. And I lay down My life for the sheep. And I have **other sheep that are not of this courtyard**; it is necessary for Me to bring these also. And they will hear My voice, and there will become one flock — one shepherd." -John 10:14-16

While the reconciliation to God began with and will forever center on chosen and set-apart Israel (the sheep who are of the good shepherd's courtyard), God's ultimate aim since the beginning has always been *everyone* who will believe — and that includes, by definition, *Gentiles* (the "other sheep" who are brought in from another pen).

The prophet says "it is too slight a thing" for Adonai's messianic servant to raise up and bring Israel back to Him. He must also do something even greater than that: namely, to be "a light of *the* Gentiles" and God's "salvation to the end of the earth" (Isaiah 49:6).[58] In that day, the Messiah—the "root of Jesse"—will stand "as a standard for *the* peoples" and all "*the* nations will look to him" (11:10).[59] The God of Israel will be "sought by those who had not asked" for Him, "found by those who had not looked" for Him, and revealed "to a nation that had not called on" His Name (65:1).[60] Through the sacrifice of Israel's Messiah—and eventually through the reconciliatory priestly service of His Jewish people — the prophet's words are fulfilled. The created ones become fully reunited with their Creator as the light of Yeshua is shone expressly to the Gentiles. Again the prophet says,

> "Look! My servant, I uphold him, My chosen one *in whom* My soul has delighted, I have put My Spirit upon him; He will bring forth *just* judgment to the nations.... This *is what* God says... 'I, ADONAI, have called you in righteousness, And I will take hold of your hand and I will guard you, And I will give you for a covenant of the people, And **a light to the Gentiles**...'" -Isaiah 42:1-6[61]

Unorthodox Evidence

This singular mission—enacted and exemplified by Israel's Messiah, to be ultimately carried out by His Jewish nation—repairs and restores the whole world. Gentiles who see this light and accept Yeshua as Messiah are no longer separated from Israel's God, but are given the authority to become

---

[58] Fulfilled, Acts 13:47.
[59] Fulfilled, Romans 15:8-12.
[60] Fulfilled, Romans 10:20.
[61] Fulfilled, Luke 2:27-32, Acts 26:22-23, cf. John 8:12.

His children (John 1:12)—*just as are the Jews*. Through Yeshua, Gentiles become fully reconciled, brought near to God, permitted to enter His presence, completely sanctified, and—perhaps most astoundingly—made co-beneficiaries of the promises that God covenanted solely with Israel. Though the post-biblical (and sometimes Jew-loathing) religious institution of *Christianity* would eventually be established by men, Yeshua's salvation of innumerable individual Gentile *Christians* was instituted by divine design.

> Therefore, remember that at one time, you, the Gentiles in the flesh... were at that time apart from Messiah, having been alienated from the citizenship of Israel, and strangers to the covenants of the promise, having no hope and without God in the world. But now, in Messiah Yeshua, you—being at one time far off—became near in the blood of the Messiah. For He is our peace, who made *the* both [Jew and Gentile] one, and broke down the middle wall of the enclosure... so that in Him He might create the two into one new man, making peace, and might reconcile both in one body to God through the *execution* stake, having killed the hostility by it. And having come, He proclaimed Good News: peace to you—the Far-off [the Gentiles]—and peace to the Near [the Jews], for through Him we have the access to the Father—we both—in one Spirit. -Ephesians 2:11-18

The Jewish people are uniquely advantaged to be "near" to God. We have the covenants, the circumcision, and even the Messiah—every benefit of our natural birthright. God's intention for the Gentiles, then, was for them to also be brought near, like Israel, *despite* their innate disadvantage of being "far off." Through Yeshua, Gentiles are now able to join with believing Israel in the household of God (2:19), and together we both have equal access to the Father.

What has transpired over the last two thousand years, however, is a Christian religion actively and perpetually usurping the God-ordained place of the people of Israel. While it is actually Gentiles who are by nature distant from Israel's God, needing Yeshua to bring them near to both Jewish believers and to Himself, Christianity has flipped the script. Instead, Christianity now sees itself as the true household of faith, and believes that anyone seeking salvation must therefore be converted into it—including Jews. Though the prophesied and promised mass salvation of the Gentiles was supposed to cause Yeshua-rejecting Jews to be provoked to a godly jealousy (Romans 11:11), Christianity has succeeded mainly in merely provoking them. It is no surprise, then, that historically—and regrettably, even now—Jews have wanted nothing to do with the allegedly separate and pagan God of the Christians. And yet, our great God can overcome even the Gentiles' longtime conceit and mishandling of their spiritual riches in order to bring all His plans to completion. Christians who are arrogant toward Jews—especially antisemitic ones—will be condemned.

> But I speak to you—to the Gentiles... be not high-minded, but be fearing, for if God did not spare the natural [Jewish] branches, otherwise, He will also not spare you.... you will also be cut off.... For I do not want you to be ignorant of this mystery, brothers, so that you may not be wise in your own conceits: that hardness in part has happened to Israel until the fullness of the Gentiles comes in; and so all Israel will be saved.... –Romans 11:13-26

The vast number of Gentiles throughout history who have believed in the Messiah of Israel is consequently not a reason for

Jews to reject Him (even though their belief has been based in part on an unscriptural replacement of the Jewish people, as well as an anti-Jewish mischaracterization of the person and teachings of the true Jewish Yeshua). Rather, the widespread belief of the Gentiles is *evidence* that Yeshua is in fact the prophesied Messiah of Israel. The historical Jewish rejection of Yeshua was self-inflicted — a "hardness in part" that was further entrenched and exacerbated by an antagonistic, arrogant Christianity. Yet in the end, it will be the "fullness of the Gentiles"—those who not only claim Israel's God, but who love and work to restore His chosen people—that will cause Jewish hearts to soften and open toward their long lost brother Yeshua, "and so all Israel will be saved." As Jews, we need to acknowledge God's promised reconciliation among the Gentiles, look past—and even forgive—the conceit and hate and error of Christianity toward the Jewish people, and then reclaim both our Messiah and our vocational legacy as a light of salvation to the nations.

Restoring the Gospel According to Israel

To my Gentile brothers and sisters in Messiah, then, know that this long-awaited reconciliation of the world through the Jewish people now paradoxically begins with you. The Gospel according to Israel has been historically and systematically suppressed, obscured, altered and interrupted, such that it is now your responsibility to return and reinstate it to those for whom it was originally intended. The Good News of Yeshua is forever yours. You are not expected to surrender it, nor to minimize your own significance or importance in it, nor to separate yourself from the Messiah who loves you and calls you His own. Yet the faith you have inherited spawns largely from a Christianity that is in many ways hostile to the very people who brought you that faith. Your grief, accordingly, is invited; your humble kindness, required. Take to heart the fullness of the Gospel according to Israel, and then see the world's need — and even your own — to reach the Jewish people for Messiah. Help reignite the smoldering fire, help make the dry bones come alive, help re-graft the broken-off branches, and make Israel jealous with your humility, your compassion, your testimony, and your knowledge of the truth that their enshrouded King and Messiah is, indeed, Yeshua.

And to my Jewish brothers and sisters — now that you are rightly acquainted with our people's story and our purpose in the plans of God — accept today your ancient birthright and eternal destiny as the righteous remnant of Israel. The Gospel according to Israel is uniquely our message. It came to us first. God set us apart not as individuals but as a group — as a holy people — for the stated purpose of carrying that very message to the nations. And our continued existence — despite thousands of years of assimilation, ostracizing and persecution — is a living testament that every word of our God is true. As Jews, then, we alone are singularly called, qualified and equipped to share not only our own story, but the salvation of our own Messiah. God's reconciliation of the world through the covenants He made exclusively with us is not incidental to the Gentiles' deliverance. Nor was the Good News ever meant to be presented to the Gentiles in a vacuum, forsaking the contexts of Israel's priesthood and of God's everlasting covenantal relationship with His Jewish people. Therefore, despite two millennia of history, religion, appropriation and tradition, we must transcend and devote ourselves to fulfilling the God-given purpose of our very existence. We were made for the explicit intent of shining the light of the true Yeshua to the world as a testimony to all the Gentiles... "and then will the end arrive" (Matthew 24:14).

Restoring the Gospel according to Israel—bringing it to a people and a world that want nothing to do with it—will require you to first relinquish your own preconceptions, and then to humbly bow your thoughts and conclusions to the perfect word of God. Be convinced of Scripture's truth in the face of long-standing convention, and then allow it to rewrite the understanding of your heart so that you may proclaim it in fullness to every ear God makes ready to hear.

May the loving-kindness, peace and unmerited favor from our God be yours abundantly in the Master Yeshua. May you forever follow Him down the narrow path of life, walking not in the darkness, but in the unquenchable, inextinguishable light of the world.

> And the city [New Jerusalem] has no need of the sun nor the moon, that they may shine on it, for the glory of God gives off its light, and the lamp of it is the Lamb. And the nations will walk by its light... –Revelation 21:23-24

APPENDIX

What Is the Good News?

This appendix contains brief summaries of each chapter of the book. Its purpose is to provide you with a concise overview of the *Gospel According to Israel* for your quick reference.

GOD OF CREATION

The Good News starts at the beginning.

In the beginning, God spoke all things into existence. Through His Word, He made everything, and He made it good. Without God, we would have nothing, and be nothing. He is the Creator and Giver of all life, worthy of abundant gratitude, blessing and honor.

GOD OF JUDGMENT

The Good News gives us a choice.

When God created the first man, Adam, they walked closely with one another. Everything was perfect. Having set Adam in a garden paradise, God gave him just one command and one choice: to obey Him, remain close to Him, and live forever; or to disobey Him, be separated from Him, and die. But Adam and his wife gave in to their desires and made the choice to sin. They defied God's command, bringing judgment and death upon themselves—and upon everyone who would come after them. Banished because of their sin, with the garden gate shut behind them, mankind was now permanently separated from their Creator. Humanity needed a way to be reconciled to God.

GOD OF SALVATION

The Good News rides on a perfect rescue vessel.

The descendants of Adam increased in their depravity, grieving their Creator. So great was their wickedness that God determined to wipe them out—all of them—in an apocalyptic flood. And yet, one man remained whom God found to be righteous. So, initiating His plan to restore humanity to Himself, God chose Noah and his family for the preservation of all mankind. Into an ark designed by God, Noah entered through its narrow door and was saved from the flood of destruction. God then promised to never again flood the earth, and Noah's offspring repopulated the world.

GOD OF PROMISE

The Good News keeps its commitments.

After many generations, God called to the man Abraham—whose wife was barren—telling him to leave his father's home. God promised that He would give Abraham a land not his own, and a great many descendants through whom all the families of the earth would be blessed. Abraham responded in faith, and in his and his wife's very old age, God kept His word.

Born to Abraham was Isaac, the son of the promise; and from Isaac came tenacious Jacob, whom God gave the name Israel. Through the patriarchs and the promises God made to His chosen nation, the plan to restore all peoples was carefully being laid.

THE GOD OF ISRAEL: GOD OF DELIVERANCE

The Good News finishes what it begins.

Famine led the fledgling House of Jacob from the Land of his fathers into Egypt. There they prospered and multiplied until a new king arose and forced them into centuries of hard slavery. But God had not forgotten His promise to His people. He heard their cries and raised up the deliverer, Moses. Through His servant, and with great signs and wonders, God showed His power to Israel's oppressors. Finally, after being crushed by a plague of death, Egypt relented to God, and let His people go. God saved Israel from that destruction by the life of innocent lambs—with blood painted on the doorways of their homes. Establishing a pattern of things to come, instantly, they were set free, leaving Egypt—and their slavery to it—behind forever.

THE GOD OF ISRAEL: GOD OF COMMANDMENTS

The Good News comes with instructions.

God remembered and delivered His chosen nation in service to His master plan. In fulfillment of the promise made to their fathers—that they would be a blessing to the world—the people of Israel were to serve as the national facilitator of humanity's restoration to their Creator. Yet to be that holy mediator before

God, unique among the nations, Israel needed to wholly love God, listen only to His voice, and learn the difference between right and wrong. And so, through His servant Moses, God gave Israel His special instructions and commands — His Torah. Though God knew His chosen people would quickly turn away and sin, their calling nevertheless required them to be a righteous and holy people.

THE GOD OF ISRAEL: GOD OF ATONEMENT

The Good News requires endless sacrifice.

Sin would plague the people of Israel, as it has all humanity since the beginning, keeping them estranged from God. Since sin still carried the ultimate price of death, atonement needed to be made. In order for the people to be forgiven and cleansed from their sin, God established His intercessory priesthood and system of substitutionary sacrifice. Yet no matter how many innocent animals were slain, the people's ceaseless offenses made it impossible for that blood to take away their sins forever. The mediation of the priests, being marred by their own sin, could only bring temporary and partial relief. Endless sin would require unending atonement. God was planning an even greater priesthood and more perfect sacrifice to release people from their sins once and for all.

GOD OF FAITHFULNESS

The Good News never gives up on you.

After a year of preparation and instruction, God led the people of Israel to the edge of the promised Land. But upon finding it occupied, they refused to enter and take their inheritance as instructed. Instead, the people rose up against Moses, inciting God to sentence that generation to a long, slow death in the desert. Yet despite Israel's grumbling, God remained faithful and refused to give up on them. Through Moses, God continually provided for the needs of a broken people who so often—and so easily—broke faith with Him. Even after the death of their deliverer, God did not let them down. He promised to raise up from their brothers a savior and prophet like Moses in whose mouth would also be the word of God.

GOD OF REDEMPTION

The Good News humbles disobedience, and forgives.

The following generation finally entered the promised Land. There, they repeatedly turned away to worship other gods, prompting the one true God to allow their enemies to defeat them. When the people cried out for help, God would save them, but then they would forget Him again. Eventually, they rejected God as their king and demanded a man to rule over them instead. So God gave the people the arrogant and oppressive ruler they deserved. But when that king cast aside God's commands, God raised up a new leader to replace him—one whom Israel did not deserve. With the humble king David, God forgave and redeemed the people's evil plea, and made an everlasting covenant with David and his descendants. A son of David would sit on the throne of Israel forever—an endless kingdom ruled by the redemptive hand of an eternal king... the king of Israel, the Messiah.

GOD OF REVELATION

The Good News reveals the end from the beginning.

Israel would continue to lose their way, and eventually lose their land as well. Yet despite the failing state of their national, priestly purpose, God remained faithful, continually speaking to them through His prophets. As they admonished the people to turn from their evil and wickedness, the prophets also revealed a far-off figure who would restore Israel—and the entire world—to their God. They said this Messiah would come from the line of David—that He would be a prophet, priest and king. They said He would be pierced for our violations, yet despised and rejected by His people. They said that God would call Him His Son. They said He would save us from our sins. Since the moment the garden gate slammed shut, each doorway that God had opened would lead Israel—and humanity—back here.

GOD OF LOVE

The Good News gives until there is nothing left to give.

In the beginning was the Word—who was with God, and was God—yet He humbled Himself and became a human being. The Messiah Yeshua, the goal of God's salvation plan, had finally come to His Jewish people. Despite sharing our human nature, Yeshua was nevertheless guiltless, and lived His entire life without sin. As an upholder of Torah, He taught the people about God's judgment, His eternal promised land, and the narrow door one must pass through to get there. Filled with power, Yeshua travelled throughout the Land of Israel healing the sick, giving sight to the blind, and promising the forgiveness of sins. But when many in Israel followed Him, the religious leaders perceived Him as a threat and conspired to have Him killed.

Though He had done no wrong, Yeshua willingly gave Himself up to die as a self-sacrificial substitute, so that everyone who believes in Him may have life everlasting. Death, however, could not hold the Son of God, and on the third day, Yeshua rose from the dead in eternal victory over sin and death. Through Yeshua's shed blood, God made a New Covenant with His people Israel. By that perfect, once-and-for-all atonement, all sins are forgotten, and all guilt and shame are wiped away. The Messiah Yeshua—the King of Israel, the Lamb of God—loved us and gave Himself for us so that the final door of salvation could be opened. Humanity's long-awaited, promised restoration to our Creator was, at long last, complete.

GOD OF RECONCILIATION

The Good News returns us to God.

The Good News is a Jewish story about the Jewish people and their Jewish Messiah whom the God of Israel sent to repair the world. Yeshua's reconciling work to restore humanity's relationship with God is embedded in the story and covenants of Israel's very own Scriptures. Not only does Yeshua make a way for all who believe to turn to God, He also restores the Jew to his long-lost, ancient function as Israel: to be a light of salvation for the world. In Messiah, we are made brand new, able to return to God and walk with Him in the newness of life. Like Israel leaving Egypt, we are no longer enslaved to our past. Through Yeshua, God forgives what we owe, forgets it for good, and receives us to Himself in full reconciliation.

GOD OF LIFE

The Good News makes all things new.

When we are in Yeshua, we are reborn a new creation: the old has gone; the new has come (2 Corinthians 5:17). What, then, must you now do?

To be saved, you must first believe. "If you confess with your mouth, 'Yeshua is Master,' and believe in your heart that God raised Him out of the dead, you will be saved" (Romans 10:9).

To be forgiven, you must repent. "Repent, therefore, and return, for the blotting out of your sins, so that times of refreshing may come from the presence of ADONAI" (Acts 3:19f).

And to be reconciled to your Creator, you must die to your old ways and turn from your sin. "Therefore, O house of Israel, I will judge you each according to his ways.... Return and turn yourselves back from all your violations, and then guilt will not be a stumbling-block to you. Throw off from yourselves all your violations by which you have sidestepped, and make to yourselves a new heart and a new spirit" (Ezekiel 18:30-31).

Enter in through the door of Yeshua, and receive the erasure of your shame. Be made new and reconciled to God. Come now to Yeshua... and choose life.

About the Author

Kevin Geoffrey, born Kevin Geoffrey Berger, is the firstborn son of a first-generation American, non-religious, Jewish family. Ashamed of his lineage from childhood, he deliberately attempted to hide his identity as a Jew, legally changing his name as a young adult. After experiencing an apparently miraculous healing from an incurable disease, Kevin began to search for God. Eventually, he accepted Yeshua as Messiah, a decision which would ultimately lead him to be restored to his Jewish heritage. Today, Kevin is a strong advocate for the restoration of all Jewish believers in Yeshua to their distinct calling and identity as the faithful remnant of Israel.

Kevin is an ordained teacher through the Messianic Jewish Movement International (MJMI). He has been involved in congregational planting, faith-community development, and itinerant teaching, but is best known as a writer, having authored ten books to date, including the *Messianic Daily Devotional* and *Bearing the Standard: A Rallying Cry to Uphold the Scriptures*. Kevin is also the editor of the *Messianic Jewish Literal Translation of the New Covenant Scriptures (MJLT NCS)*. In addition to teaching about uniquely Messianic Jewish topics, Kevin's clear and impassioned messages focus on true discipleship, radical life-commitment to Yeshua, and upholding the Scriptures as God's perfect standard.

Kevin is a husband, a father, and also the principal laborer of both Perfect Word Ministries and MJMI. He currently lives in Phoenix, Arizona with Esther, his wife of more than twenty-five years, with whom he has four cherished sons, Isaac, Josiah, Hosea, and Asher.

If you are Jewish

and have chosen to believe that Yeshua is the Messiah—or even if you're still not sure—we invite you to reach out to us today for further guidance or help.

email | contact@mjmi.org
text | 515-999-6564
toll free | 800-4YESHUA

Other Books by Perfect Word Publishing

Messianic Daily Devotional

Messianic Mo'adiym Devotional

Messianic Torah Devotional

The Messianic Life:
Being a Disciple of Messiah

Deny Yourself: The Atoning
Command of Yom Kippur

Behold the Lamb (Passover Haggadah)

The Real Story of Chanukah

Bearing the Standard: A Rallying Cry to Uphold the Scriptures

Messianic Jewish Literal Translation of the
New Covenant Scriptures (MJLT NCS)

That I May Gain Messiah:
A Messianic Jewish Devotional

Not By Faith Only:
Messianic Jewish Discipleship from the Book of James

resources.perfectword.org

1-888-321-PWMI

PERFECT *Word*
P·U·B·L·I·S·H·I·N·G

A ministry of Perfect Word Ministries

www.ingramcontent.com/pod-product-compliance
Lightning Source LLC
Chambersburg PA
CBHW070452100426
42743CB00010B/1587